THE SUBTERRANEAN ECONOMY

THE SUBTERRANEAN ECONOMY

Dan Bawly

McGraw-Hill Book Company

New York St. Louis San Francisco Auckland Bogotá Hamburg Johannesburg London Madrid Mexico Montreal New Delhi Panama Paris São Paulo Singapore Sydney Tokyo Toronto

Library of Congress Cataloging in Publication Data

Bawly, Dan, (date)

The subterranean economy.

Includes index.
1. Tax evasion. 2. Informal sector (Economics)
I. Title.
HJ2348.5.B38 336.24'16 81–12425
AACR2

1 2 3 4 5 6 7 8 9 0 DODO 8 9 8 7 6 5 4 3 2

ISBN 0-07-004153-9

The editors for this book were Kiril Sokoloff and Christine M. Ulwick, the designer was Elliot Epstein, and the production supervisor was Sally Fliess. It was set in Melior by DataPage, Inc.

Printed and bound by R.R. Donnelley & Sons Company.

In memory of
LAZARE
Friend, partner,
teacher, father,
with whom I shared
this and other adventures

Contents

PREFACE

Sometime in the early 1970s, it became clear to me that capitalism, at least as operated in the more or less social welfare democracies, was in serious trouble. At first, I suspected it was the sickness of an interim period of economic adjustment, prolonged by the revolution in the price of fuel and energy after the 1973 Yom Kippur War.

But gradually I realized that the economic malady of the West was more serious, that it had been exacerbated and could become chronic owing to the failure of Western governments to comprehend the emergence of the modern subterranean economy.

The subterranean economy would never have reached its present degree of power had it not been for the presumptuous attempts of postwar governments to eradicate poverty through "big government" welfare programs and mismanaged high taxation policies. True, some countries can boast that they hardly have an economically deprived stratum in their society; but this is thanks to inherently healthy growth, endangered, rather than helped, by big government.

The Subterranean Economy is about the unmeasured economy of open society, second in size only to the entire recorded output of the West, possibly almost as large as the published production figures for the whole of the United States. The book describes how this economy arose and became such a dominant factor and goes on to assess why, where, and by whom tax avoidance and evasion are practiced.

The realization that big government, with its heavy social welfare commitment relying on an overambitious tax program, is not performing as might have been hoped leads to the discovery that the administration has undertaken too many responsibilities and thereby has lost its bearings. The public is gradually turning to passive resistance, declaring less and less of its income in tax returns. Avoision — a hybrid term for the combination of avoidance and evasion — is becoming a common phenomenon. How avoision is practiced in both a cash and barter economy, with the apparent, if passive, support of financial institutions in all sectors of the national and multinational economies, is the main thrust of the second half of the book.

The Subterranean Economy describes how muddled bureaucratic management makes people rebel against the internal revenue system. It then tells of modern tax avoidance and evasion practices on both sides of the Atlantic and how legal and illegal ways of reducing one's tax burden intertwine.

It is aimed at the poor, the middle class, and the wealthy; senior executives and young moonlighters; officers of public companies; owners of very private businesses; globetrotters; and, above all, honest taxpayers, that still silent majority who unquestioningly accept self-assessment and naively believe that everybody else does, too.

In conclusion, I recommend that the free society substantially reduce and simplify taxation rates, as well as cut government involvement in national economies by half or more.

Dan Bawly
August 1981

Acknowledgments

Collecting material for *The Subterranean Economy* was an instructive experience. Many of those whom I approached for advice or assistance helped gladly, cooperating far more extensively than I had expected.

It all began early in 1974, when the observations on the subject of Dr. Ben Ami Zuckerman, then assistant to the Israeli Commissioner of Revenue, persuaded me to investigate the size of this economy.

In June 1979, after I had prepared a short paper on the subject, Clifford Barclay and his son Stephen invited me to discuss it with a number of successful businesspeople, eminent academicians, and a Liberal Rabbi, at the Reform Club in London. They were most encouraging. Later, having also read the paper, Sir Sigmund Warburg wrote to me suggesting it be developed into a book.

Across the Atlantic, O.B. Hardison, director of the Folger Shakespeare Library in Washington, and Martin Krasney of the Aspen Institute for Humanistic Studies were both very interested in the subject and encouraged me as I set out on the adventure. Daniel Seligman of *Fortune* magazine was of help.

Kiril Sokoloff is responsible for *The Subterranean Economy* being published at this moment. His interest and pressure for a tight timetable convinced me that I should go ahead with the venture.

Among those who helped me were many of my associates at Horwath & Horwath International.

The past and present presidents of the American firm of Laventhol & Horwath, Robert Ferst and George Bernstein, encouraged me in the undertaking. Stanley Ferst of Philadelphia was interested; his help in collecting material was invaluable from the start. He was aided by Ed O'Grady, John Lesure, and Al Ellentuck. In New York, Martin Helpern contributed color and insight. It is thanks to him that Arthur Gelber, aided by B. Fisch, prepared the Appendix describing most of the tax forms that sole proprietorships in New York City have to consider filling. In Toronto, Canada, Harvey Hecker devoted much time to my project and contributed excellent raw material. There were Edward (Teddy) L. Langton, who heads Stoy Horwath in England and his assistant, Mary Rose Sconce, as well as his partners, Peter Darnell and Phillip Sober. They were among the first to send me material about the underground economy in the United Kingdom. They were soon followed by Philippe Gendraud and Rene Amirkhanian of Horwath & Horwath, France, and Aldo Sanchini of Horwath & Horwath, Italia, as well as Harry Boland and Peter Carton of Horwath, Haughey, Boland and Company, Ireland. Also, Reinhard Imhof from Horwath & Gelbert in Germany.

Sven-Erik Johansson of Horwath & Horwath, Sweden, was most kind in arranging a "tutorial" for me on conditions in his country. They included a long conference with Lennart Bjerkner and another with Dag Victor and Anders Leijon. Sven-Erik was aided by two partners, Bertil Jonsson and Ake Edberg, whom he invited for different sessions.

Later, Pieter Kraan in the Netherlands was of much help. He arranged for Dr. Jan Simons to spend a day taking me to Professor Arnold Heertje. In Brussels, Marcel Tinnemans and Professor Walter Missorten were equally eager to contribute. And Ruedi Fleischmann, who heads Horwath Treuhand & Revisions AG in Zurich, introduced me to Dr. Bruno Becchio, a brilliant and lively lawyer.

Juan Seif of Venezuela, Ramon Espejo of Chile, and the

brothers Salvador Francisco and Joao Paulo Conti of Brazil all offered Latin American insights.

A special note of appreciation is due to V.M. Raiji of Bombay, India. The material he offered on the black economy in his country was fascinating and, for me, an eye-opener.

Others outside Horwath & Horwath were very helpful, such as Professor Ed Feige, from the Netherlands Institute of Advanced Studies in Wassenaar, who has been doing serious, in-depth microeconomic research into the phenomenon.

In London, I picked the brains of many excellent people. To name a few: Arthur Seldon of the Institute for Economic Affairs; Lord Nathan; Sir William Pile, who was, until the end of 1979, chairman of the board of Inland Revenue in the United Kingdom; Barbara Shenfield, who had a lot of interesting points on the subject, both orally and in writing; and The Rt. Hon. Maurice Macmillan, M.P.

Then, in Copenhagen, I met with Mogens Glistrup, one of the few who have come out in public for the end of income tax. His call triggered the birth of a large and vocal political party. In Geneva, I spent some time with a lawyer and long-standing friend, Michel Halperin.

Eddy Feitsma helped me with my Dutch, and there were others who shared their thoughts with me, whose ideas I poached but who, for various legitimate and sensible reasons, preferred to remain anonymous. Their insights and knowledge were very important and I am correspondingly grateful.

There were those who helped me in Israel. Eliahu Salpeter, a fine, balanced journalist and wise friend offered sound, constructive critique; his advice prevented me from making a number of silly mistakes and added color and good sense. Penina Barkai spent weeks patiently typing and retyping the manuscript, gently editing, preventing some errors, suggesting subtle changes and improvements as we worked. Miranda Kaniuk provided her assured editing, sensitive observations, fine corrections, and inspiring comments.

It is common for a writer to thank his wife for her help. Ilon's aid was uncommon: the example of her own steady writing and rewriting, her encouraging words and attitude—these were but a few of the ways in which she was so special.

THE SUBTERRANEAN ECONOMY

1

WHAT IS IT ALL ABOUT? A PERSONAL INTRODUCTION

In 1974, a brief study put out by the Israeli Commissioner of Internal Revenue suggested that Israelis were paying 71 percent of their gross income in taxes to the government. As if some intrinsic ethical merit were attached to the payment of taxes, there was a note of pride, achievement, and satisfaction in the announcement. At a meeting with him, I asked the then assistant commissioner whether he, personally, believed that we were all really paying over two-thirds of our income to the government. If so, how could we maintain the rapid increase in our standard of living? We both agreed that the figure of total cash revenue paid into government coffers was incontestable. But I asked whether the tax collected might not be related to a figure higher than generally assumed? By way of answer, he referred me to Israel's Central Bureau of Statistics and to the Economic Research Department of the Bank of Israel. Over the following three years, I met with virtually all the bureaucrats in charge of collecting data and calculating the GNP of Israel and related statistics. Most "pooh-poohed" my argument that it was illogical to claim that if people were letting 70 percent of their income go to taxes, there must be a very large hidden economy, somewhere.

However, there were exceptions—people who did recognize that there might be a problem and thought that research into the matter was advisable. One was Dr. Meir Heth, at one time banking commissioner at the Bank of Israel and now chairman of the Tel Aviv Stock Exchange. After observing certain unexplained discrepancies between reported purchases in foreign currency and actual imports recorded in the ports of entry into Israel, he felt that the part of the gross national product might be larger than generally believed; that, not having reassessed their instruments of measurement in years, the macroeconomists might be at fault. Dr. Meir Tamari, a research fellow with the Bank of Israel and an economist, is another; he is rare among that breed in that he can relate intelligently between macro- and microeconomics.

Later, the person then in charge of Britain's Inland Revenue warned of large-scale evasion, but no operative steps were taken against it. Like the Great Wall of China, the local "imperial bureaucracy"* stood firm against any hints of dangerous growth in the unrecorded sector of the national economy.

In the late 1970s, a new, less secure government took office in Israel, and there was less certainty about the accuracy of the national accounts. Still, there was considerable resistance to any attempt to reevaluate and reassess the efficacy of the instruments of measurement of the gross national product. Paying lip service to the suggestion of a flaw in their system, the bureaucrats hired some possibly none-too-well-disciplined academics to check whether the instruments of economic measurement were adequate or needed updating. Not surprisingly, nearly three years later they were still in the preliminary stages of their research. . . .

It made me uncomfortable to see the considerable unwillingness of senior government officers to conclude that the national accounts of my country were inaccurate, and it was quite a revelation to discover that the underground economy was just as deeply rooted and just as studiously

---

* It was Norman Macrae who wrote in *The Economist* (December 23, 1978, pp. 45–54) on the crisis resulting from the abuse by government of the modern imperial bureaucracy; he charged that democratic government composed of both elected ministers and civil servants has become far more interested in defending and propagating its own political-bureaucratic establishment than in serving the public as well as it can. In the process, he said, it has come to operate at uneconomic, often exorbitant cost.

See also Professor Gordon Fullock, with Richard B. McKenzie, *The New World of Economics,* Richard D. Irwin, Illinois.

ignored in other free societies, if not more so. When, in the mid-1970s, I first asked politicians, economists, professional colleagues, and friends about the subterranean economy in their countries, they all claimed that it had a marginal presence, if any. It was only around 1978 that the subterranean economy began to be grudgingly recognized as a problem, a serious element of the national life of most western countries; but only by a few. Today, the presence of the hidden economy is widely accepted, another piece of evidence of the unhealthy state of whatever nation being discussed at the dinner table.

It was thus that I began assembling data on the subject—verbal and written. Gradually, recognition increased and quite provocative information began to reach me from associates and correspondents.

Several professional tax consultants and specialists kindly lent me their observations on the state of the subterranean economy in their countries; many of their comments are scattered throughout the various chapters of the book. An American associate wrote to say that he believes the subterranean economy is continuing to grow and is becoming more of a problem in the United States. In no place does it appear to be static. Tax evaders have multiplied to such a large extent that, in the few isolated cases in which the Internal Revenue prosecutes, it actually has no serious deterrent effect on the climate of evasion.

In describing the subterranean economy and matters related thereto, which is the main purpose of this book, I have offered a number of economic opinions and postulates commonly held, even if not accepted, by all economists. It would not have been relevant herein to expand on them or to try to prove their merits or drawbacks.

THE ROLE OF THE CERTIFIED PUBLIC ACCOUNTANT

There is a link between the subject of tax compliance and the work and services expected from the chartered public accountant. It was as an active partner in an Israeli firm of CPAs that I learned to serve clients and still do so. It was as a practicing auditor that I discovered the subterranean economy.

Independent certified public accountants have not been able to help materially in combating acts of civil disobedience to the fiscal and tax laws of today's complicated world. Their training and the instruments at their disposal do not equip them to deal with the deterioration in economic morality.

In most countries, but mainly in the English-speaking world, businesspeople and other big income earners retain independent accountants to verify their books and tax returns. As well as expressing an opinion on the way in which the financial statements are presented, independent accountants are increasingly expected to act as consultants, advising their clients how, legitimately, to avoid as much taxation as possible. In an age when bureaucratic policies are muddled and incoherent, and it is common to admire successful avoidance schemes, members of the accounting profession compete to provide new ideas of how to pay less taxes, since those who do so best will earn the most.

Apart from blatant and fully documented tax evasion, which certified public accountants would abhor and denounce, the tax authorities cannot expect any possible aid from them. As evasion increases, the demand for auditing services decreases and, certainly, for auditing services from the major accounting firms.*

HOW IS THE SUBTERRANEAN ECONOMY MADE UP?

The unmeasured economy includes the following types of activity:

Funds Derived from Criminal Action

These include funds derived from protection, organized prostitution, illegal drug trade, and various types of larceny, theft, and white-collar crime.

---

* The accounting profession has developed in the United States, the United Kingdom, and the Netherlands over more than a century and has been fed by self-regulation, public demand, and government regulation. Its deep involvement in the attempt to give what it believes to be a fair description of the affairs of its clients is considerably different from the legalistic, more formal, less searching attitude of its Latin and Germanic counterparts.

Funds Derived from Breaking Foreign Currency Control Laws

These activities mainly take the form of smuggling funds across borders. They generally take place in countries where the foreign currency reserves are limited and laws and regulations attempt to reduce to a minimum the use of unauthorized foreign currency. There are virtually no such constraints, or very few, in the western open society. Controls are, however, common and at times effective in the Communist countries. Similar, although less effective, are foreign currency controls in a large number of the South American and Asian states. South Africa and many other African republics also maintain foreign currency controls.

Funds Derived from Illegal Work

These come from work carried out by laborers with no work permit, such as illegal Mexican and other Hispanic immigrants in the southern United States and *gastarbeiter* in Europe. They include moonlighting. Such funds are common in most countries where there are either wage controls or high personal tax rates. They are prevalent in both the Communist countries and the free democracies.

Then there are also funds derived from evaded and avoided untaxed income and the following:

Funds Derived from Untaxed Extraterritorial Economic Activities

Not every member of the subterranean economy is illegally evading the payment of income taxes. A substantial number of people and, even more important, a considerable part of the money lost thereby, joins the unrecorded economy by way of clever tax planning: the use of tax shelters, tax havens (see Chapter 10), or recognized tax perks.

While the funds accrued from crime and smuggling across borders are also part of the subterranean economy, as are those derived from illegal work, their story deserves a fuller study than this book will offer. We will confine ourselves to an attempt to describe how the subterranean economy came into being, what it is about, and what good or harm it is doing.

This is not intended to be a book in which morals and morality are evaluated and judged. The book does, however, agree with Barbara Shenfield, who points out that "the undeclared economy is governed by market principles. It increases the wealth not only of its participants but also of those in the declared economy."

WHAT SHOULD WE CALL IT?

Among those aware of the covert economy, there is no consensus as to what best to call it. Before its full extent became apparent, the most common terms were the "black" or "underground" economy. Some simply called it the illegal economy. All three terms are negative, colored descriptions with certain legal implications. The phrase "hidden economy" was also used.

In recent years, as the phenomenon was better appreciated, some socioeconomists thought that a more neutral term would be apt; the "undeclared" or the "unmeasured" economy were suggested.*

Some people, with tidy minds, regard it as the parallel economy. But parallel means two bodies which are equidistant at all points, which the recorded and unrecorded economies are not. Trying to rank the economies and talking of the "second" economy is of little meaning. I was delighted to learn of the descriptive and charming "whispering" economy, but doubt whether the name will catch on. Raffaele de Grazia mentions the "twilight" economy.[1] Colorful, but how precise?

The Americans appear to have attached themselves to the term "subterranean economy." The phrase was coined by Professor Peter Gutman and first saw print at the end of 1977.[2]

The Europeans are less definite, more ambivalent, and, at the moment, mostly still stick to the terms black or underground economy.

Nor is there any one accepted and satisfactory definition of the subterranean economy. Possibly, the best is that "it is that part

---

* Norman Macrae, deputy editor of *The Economist,* quotes a former aide to President Carter in the issue for December 27, 1980, as having spoken of the "unobserved economy."

of the gross national product that is not measured by official statistics."

If this economy continues to grow, it will have to be compared to the white? aboveground? overt? declared? measured? economy.

REFERENCES

1. "Clandestine Employment: A Problem of Our Times," *International Labour Review,* Vol. 119, No. 5, September–October 1980, p. 549.

2. Professor Peter Gutman, "The Subterranean Economy," *Financial Analysts Journal,* November/December 1977.

2 THE TROUBLE IS BIG GOVERNMENT

I do not know the method of drawing up an indictment against a whole people.

—EDMUND BURKE

IS THE SUBTERRANEAN ECONOMY A CANCER?

If there is a villain in the act, it is big government. There is certainly no hero. The members of the subterranean economy are not revolutionary pioneers or idealists. If asked what they are doing or why, they might say they are fighting for survival. But many may be simply anarchists or just greedy. In many countries they are the new silent majority; in others, a large silent minority.

An exception may be Mogens Glistrup, founder, leader, and brains behind the Progress Party, the second or third in size of the dozen or so Danish political groups, represented in the Folketinget (Parliament) since 1973 and the only true Opposition party. Mr. Glistrup's platform calls for the complete phasing out of income and allied taxes over seven years, cutting down paper work and thinning out the jungle of fiscal laws.

A practicing lawyer and, in the early 1970s, considered a brilliant lecturer on fiscal law at the University of Copenhagen, Mr. Glistrup began his political career by declaring he would refuse to pay any taxes. When I met him in January 1981, he was about to vacate his home, with its indoor, fully heated, Olympic-size swimming pool, which he has had to sell for cash to pay taxes slapped on him. But he intended to continue fighting the fisc. A marzipan-munching, heavy-set, 6-foot–plus Nordic antihero, more in the mold of a martyr than a politician, the local tax authorities were prosecuting him for tax delinquency, and many Danish observers believed he would end up in jail.

The welfare state and its big government twin have created new problems, no less serious, perhaps, than those it attempted to resolve. Big government has initiated its own momentum of growth: the cost of its services keeps growing excessively as the figures of its overhead increase. It is not surprising that resistance to its present size in many democracies is digging in. What is worrying is that those responsible for affairs of state are still complacent and undisturbed about the debilitating effects of welfarism and extensive government interference in the economy of many countries, from Sweden to France.

Modern-style big government is a very recent development. Central democratic government assumed responsibility, for the first time, for the general welfare of the people in the aftermath of the Great Depression and took over its administration following World War II. The emphasis was on the services provided which, for beginners, was fair and, at first, little attention was given to the cost. If services in the new welfare state did not come up to expectations, if costs turned out to be higher than projected, it was attributed to teething troubles, soon to be outgrown.

With time, however, it was discovered that the cost of the welfare state was much greater than had been anticipated; that its thirst for additional funds in the form of taxes was close to insatiable.

The western democracies are still a long way from correcting the social mistakes made, many of them in good faith, in the past generation. Whether in an authoritarian dictatorship or in a democracy, big budgets and "big-brother" government inevitably lead to a hardening of the official arteries, to bureaucratic intransigence and inflexibility. Lord Acton suggested, some hundred years ago, that "power tends to corrupt and absolute power tends to corrupt absolutely." To which, had he lived today, he could well have added "It certainly leads to the rapid growth of the subterranean economy."

This age of rampant bureaucracy has seen a widening

credibility gap between the individual and the state. Since the age of Acton, the government of the social welfare state, oiled by its immense budget, has grown to a size no earlier administration, democratic, authoritarian, or dictatorial, dared conceive. Had the Liberal Peer been alive today and still given to aphorisms, he might have coined another phrase: the bigger the government, the more powerless the civil servant to serve. While most ministers might still use the correct jargon when addressing their constituents, the budgets are structured to serve and perpetuate the administration rather than aid the general public and improve their lot. The bureaucrat often shows arrogance, but rarely any imagination or compassion.

Possibly these extensive budgets have contributed more than any other factor to ill management and the rise of modern inflation.*

Nobody likes to pay taxes. Taxation is regarded as a forced extraction of resources, lessening the funds which would otherwise be available for spending; it conveys a sense of loss—possibly accepted in a time of relatively short-term crisis, but increasingly resented as a long-term fixture. Until a generation ago, the law only interfered in everyday life to a bearable extent, and it was reasonable to expect a person of average intelligence to be aware of existing tax legislation. In spite of the inconvenience and the cost of taxes, the so-called establishment and the recognized bourgeoisie—the absolute numbers of which were limited—preferred to be law-abiding, taxpaying citizens. It was the inevitable cost of belonging to the club of respectability.

In recent years, these mores have changed. The number of laws passed, the cumbersomeness of tax computations, the complicated paperwork, the increasing incompetence of the law enforcement officers, and, particularly, the continuing high tax rates have all contributed to the growth of the popular, subterranean, covert economy, in which it is acceptable not only to avoid, but also to evade, payment of taxes on what is, legally speaking, taxable income.

---

* At the end of the 1970s, aware of the danger that runaway inflation can ultimately lead to violent social unrest and even war, the British and then the Americans voted for new leadership committed to reducing taxes and budgets substantially. But, once in power, the new leaders found that this particular task was, possibly, the most difficult they faced.

Inflation, caused mainly by the increased size of government budgets and the jump in energy costs following the repeated rises in the price of oil since 1973, has accelerated the activities of the covert economy.

Elhanan Schlesinger, chief accountant of the Israeli Securities Authority in Jerusalem, points out that the English word "value" is cognate with the Latin *valere*—to be strong, to be worth something. The Oxford dictionary notes that value is, *inter alia,* "the material or monetary worth of a thing; the amount at which it may be estimated in terms of some medium of exchange . . ." It is also the "worth of worthiness [of persons] in respect of rank or personal qualities . . . ," and the dictionary observes that in a period of inflation there is a tied, pegged erosion in the value of the latter as the cost of the former increases (*The Shorter Oxford English Dictionary,* 3d ed., Clarendon Press, Oxford, 1973). Mr. Schlesinger, a moral man, observes that today we are witnessing a rapid decline in the worth of both values.

The rise of this subterranean economy is one of the more ominous expressions of lack of confidence in government. That politicians and civil servants alike have all but ignored it reflects clearly on their sense of priorities. Their complacency seems quite extraordinary; countries cannot afford this very rapid pace of polarization between society and the state. The imperial bureaucracy is responsible for introducing and maintaining a cumbersome tax system at horrendously high rates, and for failing to get the whole population to accept it. As they opt for the undeclared economy, the evasive public is also moving rapidly toward a subterranean state. This is something no democracy can afford.

Today's subterranean economy has developed to a very high degree the art of whitewashing and laundering its funds. A far greater proportion of it than generally realized is funneled through financial institutions, rather than being transferred in ready cash. One suspects, although it has not been proven, that financial institutions and banks sometimes knowingly aid and abet the subterranean economy. Behind the Etablissements and Anstalts in Lichtenstein and Luxembourg, the funny-named companies in Panama, the Dutch Antilles, the Cayman Islands, and the Bahamas, trust accounts are kept and other forms of investments maintained with little likelihood of being traced to their real owners.*

Bearer documents of all possible sorts, such as stocks and shares, bonds, debentures, and notes, often traded through banks or brokers in the name of nominees, may be derived from untaxed income. The names of phantom businesses and fictitious persons are more common than ever. It is difficult, if not impossible, to uncover the true identity of these ghosts. As transactions become more sophisticated and more numerous, neither the bank officers nor the revenue assessing inspectors are capable, with their present modes of operation, of knowing which investments or other forms of fund flows are derived from legitimate businesses and which emanate, freshly laundered, from illicit earnings.

The subterranean economy has been growing at a more rapid pace than the open economy for some time, but it was considered to be in bad taste to talk about it, unless in connection with the fringes of society.

And then, suddenly, toward the end of the 1970s, the underground economy became an accepted subject. In mid-January 1980, for instance, several guests on the CBS program "60 Minutes" described how they had bypassed large amounts of income when preparing their tax returns. And they talked in full view of the television cameras, as though they had nothing to fear from the IRS or anybody else.[1] Not paying taxes had become respectable or, at least, almost so.

F. A. Hayek has noted how, in totalitarian states, the lawbreaker always seems to engender sympathy.[2] A similar understanding is now felt for tax criminals; even if caught (and certainly when they manage to remain undiscovered) no social stigma is attached to them.

The subterranean economy cannot be controlled by harsher suppression. Anyone who has compared notes with the experience of the Soviet Union or any of its satellites will know that such an attempt would be doomed. The number of

---

* The notion that very many people are probably involved in these undertakings was reinforced in 1978, when a senior official at Citicorp of New York charged that funds were marked up and channeled through the bank from France to a tax haven in the Caribbees. (See Chapter 9, p. 82.)

tax inspectors and government informers behind the Iron Curtain is substantially higher than in the West. Punishment for those discovered is far more severe. But evasion is no less common; probably more so.

The number of people who are liable for taxes is approximately equal to those with voting rights. With tax evasion being as tenacious as it is, enforcement by government, in the face of popular passive resistance, is not a formidable task, it is an impossible one.[3] Society no longer expects its members, as it did a generation ago, to partake wholeheartedly in the process of government and to pay all the taxes required by law. Restoring the trust of the public in the system and active, voluntary compliance with civic statutes will be a far more difficult challenge than the leadership of today realizes.

It was 1980 before staid, conservative international bodies showed any interest in the subterranean economy. Late that year, the International Labor Organization in Geneva came out with a report on moonlighting. It recognized that this factor will, inevitably, affect the character of society. Earlier, a publication of the International Monetary Fund gave it some publicity.[4] Even then, the recognition was only partial, describing the relatively primitive cash economy, but not the elements making use of national and multinational banking facilities. According to Professor Tanzi, virtually all democracies are affected by the subterranean economy and recognize it. In his colorful Latin style, Professor Tanzi adds that the unmeasured economy is "like the wind . . . hidden to the eye, but . . . very much felt." He refers to the 1977 report of the Deutsche Bundesbank that had noted that "cash payment is unquestionably gaining ground. . . ."

More international groups, ranging from the Organization for Economic Cooperation and Development to UNESCO, are studying the factors involved.

WHY THE DISENCHANTMENT WITH GOVERNMENT?

Until very recently, western countries, led by the United States and Britain, maintained a price-stable economy and a political system that enabled democracy to flourish. For over a century, the western open society, which provided both for the freedom of the individual and for social mobility, gave people a sense of security and optimism. They accepted the Judeo-Christian ethic in which they had been brought up that if one worked hard and honestly one would surely see the fruits of one's toil. It was economically and morally convenient to stay within the system because, with brief interruptions of economic recession or wars, it operated. It worked to the economic benefit of the individual and strengthened the moral fiber of both the individual and society as a whole.

In most nations, there have always been elements that chose to stay out of the declared economy. More surprising than the presence of the subterranean economy is the fact that it took so long to arrive. Part of the explanation is that, although *horrendous* tax rates have been imposed on the higher income earners for some forty years, these were invariably accompanied by very substantial perks and shelters for the preferred and privileged. They ranged from special oil depletion allowances and various types of stock options to fat expense accounts offered to the influential executive. Most members of the wealthy bourgeoisie did not have to resort to illegal evasion. Legal avoidance schemes satisfied them. [On the distinction between evasion and avoidance, see Chapter 6, p. 47.] Still, it was both the rates and the schemes that, together, led to the development of a new type of economic crime: tax fraud. The phenomenon in its present form and size is fairly recent.

Modern open society has accepted the inevitability of various overt forms of civil disobedience. It has learned how to deal with and contain some of them, such as organized terror in the United States, although not with others, such as the Mafia. The subterranean economy is a less visible form of organized crime: it is civil disobedience.

Today, these are accompanied by a lack of confidence of the general public in both the elected leadership and the heads of the opposition. It is one of the more pronounced characteristics of the West in this past generation that political parties are preferred and presidents are elected not because of any sterling leadership qualities, but because they are regarded as the lesser of two evils. Soon after giving any one party its vote of confidence, there will be general disenchantment with the new government that lasts until shortly after the next election, when the cycle starts all over again.* The advent of large-scale

---

* This has been so during the terms of most of the U.S. administrations from

inflation has amplified this feeling of national instability. It is only natural that individuals, disappointed by government's failure to protect their capital, take measures to look after themselves.

REFERENCES

1. *Fortune,* March 10, 1980, p. 78.

2. F. A. Hayek, *The Constitution of Liberty,* Routledge and Kegan Paul, London, p. 438.

3. See also Arthur Seldon, "Avoision: The Moral Blurring of a Legal Distinction Without an Economic Difference," in *Tax Avoision,* IEA Readings No. 22, The Institute of Economic Affairs, London, 1979, pp. 3–12.

4. Vito Tanzi, "Underground Economy Built on Illicit Pursuits Is Growing Concern of Economic Policymakers," International Monetary Fund Survey, Washington, D.C., February 4, 1980.

President Johnson through Nixon, Ford, and Carter. In the United Kingdom, the system of alternations started a few years earlier, when Lord Douglas-Home took over from Harold Macmillan, to be followed by the Wilson, Heath, Callaghan, and Thatcher governments.

3

THE SUBTERRANEAN ECONOMY IS AS OLD AS TAXATION

Excise: a hateful tax levied upon commodities and adjudged not by the common judges of property, but by wretches hired by those to whom the excise is paid.

—DR. SAMUEL JOHNSON

Modern income taxes are barely a generation old. Yet taxes of some sort are as old as civilization.* One of the main causes of the mass emigrations, revolts, and revolutions so frequent throughout history was public reaction to the imposition of what the people believed to be unfair taxes. Passive resistance, in the form of increasing evasion, is the modern expression of such hostility.

Avoidance and evasion began as soon as taxation was first introduced. Their popularity was always directly related to the rate of taxation. The higher the tax rate, the more popular the "avoision"** schemes. In periods when tax rates were low and of little consequence, avoision was much less extensive.

The use of the term "evasion" is far older than the use of the term "subterranean economy." Modern tax historians write of evasion in Britain in the Middle Ages. During the fourteenth

---

* In the Bible, the word is first mentioned in Genesis, chapter 49, verse 15: "Issachar is a strong ass couching down between two burdens . . . and [he] became a servant unto taxes."

** An amalgam of the two words "avoidance" and "evasion." See p. 4 of *Tax Avoision,* IEA Readings No. 22. See also Chapter 6, pp. 48–49. The word was coined by Arthur Seldon, who explained it as "tax rejection that develops from avoidance to evasion in a mixture that in the taxpayers' mind is regarded as moral, even (at times) illegal."

century, the poll tax was one of the causes of the "disappearing population." B. E. V. Sabine[1] tells us how Elizabethan tax collectors complained that some people were really worth up to forty times more than the sum at which they were assessed. Matters were no better at the end of the seventeenth century. In 1692, a levy of four shillings on the pound (20 percent) was imposed for one year, to help England wage a "vigorous war" against her traditional enemy, France. It is reported that income returns were made out in the most casual manner. While partisans of William of Orange were considered generous, the opposition was guided in estimating its income by its political sympathies, which considerably reduced the take.[2]

When and how the British colonies would have asserted their independence had the British government not levied what they believed to be very high taxes is an open question. The American Revolution would certainly have taken place later and in a different form than it did just over 200 years ago. It was the Boston Tea Party of December 16, 1773, when three shiploads of tea were dumped into the harbor by citizens demonstrating against British taxation of the beverage, that sparked off the war, leading within thirty-one months to the Declaration of Independence.

An important tax in the United Kingdom at the end of the eighteenth century was the excise tax. And a wholeheartedly disliked tax it was. Smugglers were popular among all rungs of society, including the social and ruling elites. Charles Lamb is reported to have said, "I like a smuggler. He is the only honest thief. He robs nothing but the revenue, an abstraction I never particularly cared about." Samuel Pepys, secretary of the navy in that epoch, was proud to recall how he bought smuggled cloves and nutmeg.

More surprising to the prude, but in similar vein, are the words of Adam Smith, not only the first modern economist but commissioner of customs, who wrote that a "smuggler [was] a person who, though no doubt highly blameable for violating the laws of his country, is frequently incapable of violating those of natural justice, and would have been in every respect an excellent citizen, had not the laws of the country made that a crime nature never meant it to be."

If it was accepted as inevitable that evasion closely followed direct taxation, it became clear, with the first introduction of income tax in the United Kingdom in 1799, that, in fact, the two were complementary twins. And it was in the wake of this that evasion gained a more sinister connotation for the first time. Even during those early years, although rates remained virtually nominal, there were a surprising number of complaints of evasion. In a speech to Parliament in 1845, Lord John Russell charged that income tax gave rise to great frauds and to costly legal proceedings.[3]

Upon the introduction, in the 1850s, of free trade, excise taxes were reduced substantially. In 1857, the commissioner of customs reported that "with the reduction of duties and the removal of all needless and vexatious restrictions, smuggling has greatly diminished, and the public sentiments with regard to it have undergone a very considerable change. The smuggler is no longer a subject of general sympathy or a hero of romance."

It was during the Victorian age that the "tax game" developed. It was, to a large extent, a result of the general feeling that income tax was instrinsically unfair and that the public was bound to try to avoid it. Some observers believed that the inequity inherent in the Tax Act produced evasion; they thought that a revision by a level of differentiation would ensure its disappearance. The accountant Chadwick put the matter more forcibly when he reported countless cases of tax fraud, indicating, to his mind, a very keen sense of general tax unfairness.[4]

In Britain, there was just as much skepticism about the accounting profession a century ago as there is today, but the reasons have changed. Today, whereas it is clear that accountants cannot detect all the submerged income of their clients, nobody seriously calls the profession into question. But Sir Stafford Henry Northcote,* a Victorian chancellor of the exchequer, was opposed to accountants in principle; to be effective, they would have to be downright inquisitorial and thus rather less than popular.[5]

It was the period when the United Kingdom was en route to full franchise but was still governed by the "upper classes." Politics was certainly one factor which deterred a more

---

* Visitors to the British Houses of Parliament can see the life-size statue of Sir Stafford, later the Earl of Iddesleigh, in the Centre Lobby.

aggressive method of collection, and any significant increase in government authority would have been counter to the political thinking then current.

It was a matter of practical economics; low tax rates meant that the cost of enforcement could be larger than the amount of tax lost through evasion.* Thus, the real revenue loss was believed to be not material.

Tax inspectors at the turn of the century were aware of four reasons for assessments being too low. One of these was the result of inaccurate returns, filed either in good faith or otherwise. Another was simple failure to file a return. And the last two were filing a fraudulent return or appealing against an assessment. Although tax evasion has become more sophisticated, most modern methods are variations on the above themes, with failure to file probably being the most popular.

It was at around that time, when the income tax laws began to affect more people, that public opinion concerning enforcement began to be more radical and pressure to improve tax law enforcement became more urgent. There was, however, no serious attempt to curb evasion through legislation before World War I.

From the beginning of World War I to the aftermath of World War II, western governments, generally backed by their electorate, revolutionized their approach to their public responsibilities and, hence, to their budgets and sources of revenue. Of these, the proportion of direct taxes, spearheaded by income taxes, took an enormous leap forward. Evasion continued, but it became a subject for the tax inspectors and officers, rather than the general public. And thus, it was not until the late 1960s that new, wider-spread rumblings on the subject of evasion were heard. But by then, evasion had come into its own and had become a whole subterranean economy.

During the late 1970s, the newspapers, sustained as they are by juicy tidbits, reveled in scandals concerning big individual tax

---

* A case can be made that, in modern society, in which the cost of preparing for litigation has become excessive, administrations feel it is economically inadvisable even to try to persecute the moonlighting tax evader. It would be nice to entertain the thought that present-day internal revenue policy ignores the small-time evader voluntarily and on purpose.

avoision cases. The cash economy of the moonlighting society was discovered to be a permanent fixture; more and more companies and individuals were keeping funds outside their home country and away from the eyes of their fiscal authorities.

REFERENCES

1. B. E. V. Sabine, *A History of Income Tax,* George Allen & Unwin Ltd., London, 1966.
2. Ibid.
3. *Hansard* for February 17, 1845, quoted in B. E. V. Sabine, *A History of Income Tax,* George Allen & Unwin Ltd., London, 1966, p. 178.
4. *Hansard* for February 26, 1876, quoted in B. E. V. Sabine, *A History of Income Tax,* George Allen & Unwin Ltd., London, 1966, p. 179.
5. B. E. V. Sabine, *A History of Income Tax,* George Allen & Unwin Ltd., London, 1966.

4

CAN GOVERNMENTS COME TO TERMS WITH THE UNMEASURED ECONOMY?

The ease and lack of apparent opposition with which taxes were raised in the free world since World War II brought about a peaceful capital restructuring, turning democracies into welfare states. At the same time, bureaucracies have become overstaffed and their efficacy substandard. The benefits offered, in theory, by their spending of the marginal public dollar or pound sterling have, in practice, a close to zero effect. The instruments of government have become less flexible, more rigid, until many experts fear that establishing new economic policies and changing national priorities is now close to impossible. With the mushrooming of budgets to their present size, macroeconomic thinking became static. Most economists today are two-dimensional technicians, without plan or program or a serious evaluation of what the optimal, most effective tax structure for the long term should be. There are no social scientists in office or politicians who can conceive a policy as radical as, say, how to halve the government budget.

Imperial bureaucracy assumed its prerogatives after World War II, assigning to itself the power to interfere in pricing, in the size of welfare and taxation, and in the parameters of wage differentials. Without seriously assessing the social needs, the fairness, or the popularity of the system, it set up a method of plutocratic rewards which has since assumed a powerful pulse of its own, strengthened by patronage and vested interests.

Then, gradually, as inflation increased and became a more dominant factor in the economy, government found it more difficult to carry out its programs. Stretched beyond control, government tax and welfare schemes moved from the cumbersome to the incoherent. With taxes reaching beyond sensible limits and expenditure committed almost completely to the maintenance of a vast civil service, government lost its capacity to maneuver.

Theodore S. Lowi,[1] who wrote of the disappearance of the first American constitution and the arrival of the second republic, described modern government, not only in the United States but in most democracies, as a two-part model. The administrations gradually, through a series of formal actions, monopolized an activity that either used to be part of free enterprise or, perhaps, never having existed before, was created by government. They do this by financial prowess and domination in areas ranging from defense to medicine, education, and highways. As government asserts more power and authority, imagination, initiative, and the will for improvement and positive action decline, both within the administration and outside it.

One of the main reasons why bureaucracy has become so unwieldy is the establishment of a growing number of regulatory authorities, which tend to declare illegal all nongovernment activity in the monopolized sectors unless a specific government license has been granted to the applicant. These regulatory authorities operate in fields ranging from wage controls through banking and insurance licensing, to transport and communications authorizations. Other not fully visible forms of state dominance are government guarantees and underwritings which, while often substantial, are not included in the government budget until and unless they materialize.

Once the imperial bureaucracy takes over through its agencies and offices, it uses its judgment (whatever that may mean) to hand out patronage to specific individuals or groups in the areas under its supervision. This handout is often preceded by an elaborate bargaining process. As administrations grow and their bureaucracy becomes heavier, the individual is often driven to despair by the frightening red tape.

No wonder that, in our inflexible, intransigent officialdom, a good number of people decide to take the law into their own hands.

WHY REDUCE TAXES?

In the past generation, government has rarely shown any real interest in reducing tax rates. Nor, had it wanted to do so, would it probably have had the courage. Big government budgets have generated enormous bureaucracies. To reduce them would mean not only unemployment or, at least, the reallocation of staff, but also considerable discomfort for top brass, who would have to consider and decide on new priorities and what instruments of government they would be willing to do without. Rather than do that, they added regulatory instruments when seeking to attract capital for investment in, say developing or underprivileged areas; and concocted tax incentive programs which rarely prove to be long-term successes and, with few exceptions, have turned out to be bureaucratically entangling.

In theory, it was assumed that the citizens supported a tax system that would raise the funds required by the services to be provided by the government. They might, of course, prefer not to pay any taxes themselves, but, until not too long ago, accepted that this was impossible. They were willing to settle for a fair compromise in which they traded their tax liabilities for the benefit of receiving government service, though it was never ascertained whether everyone thought they were receiving fair value for their taxes.

It is not as if the economic system has collapsed or business has suddenly become all crooked. There are, of course, still very many honest business corporations and individuals whose self-assessment may be trusted implicitly. The larger of them are audited by respectable accountants. However, from Sweden to South Africa and Australia, from the United States to the United Kingdom and Israel, the number of those who have broken through the barrier of fear and are now willing to risk the dangers of getting caught in tax evasion is growing. This is in conformity with the premise that "economic activity will dive underground whenever the costs of full membership of the formal economy exceed the risks of living outside it."[2]

There are still those who claim that the range of these activities is exaggerated. Alongside the growing school of thought which blames governments for the spread of the subterranean economy, there are those who believe the media are at fault, with exaggerated descriptions of its range. Robert J. Samuelson[3] blames government agencies for giving formal recognition to black money, thus turning it into an official feature of modern society. He warns against treating today's subterranean economy too seriously, against turning the tax evader into a maverick, with the implied conclusion that the honest taxpaying citizen is a naive fool. However, he belongs to a rapidly dwindling school.

ON THE TOLERABLE LEVEL OF TAXES

Macroeconomists speak of the "tolerable" (others call it "critical") level of public expenditure. It is the level above which expenditure may damage national economic performance and curtail growth. Similarly, if taxes rise beyond a tolerable rate, resistance from the taxpayers to financing public expenditure will rapidly increase.

It has been contended that the tolerable level will rise when real growth will have satisfied private demand.[4] Based on this assumption, at a time of real GNP growth, the critical percentage of public expenditure will tend to rise. One of the serious economic problems of the 1970s was that national economic growth, in most democracies, came close to a standstill, while public expenditure continued to grow. In most cases, this growth had probably crossed the line of tolerance several years earlier and begun encroaching on the demands of the private sector.* Government expenditure, notwithstanding the leveling off of the economy, continued to increase its level of consumption.

When World War II was nearing its end, economists and sociologists were thinking ahead as to what should be the limit of public expenditure in the postwar period. Dr. Colin Clark of Australia and the United Kingdom believed that where taxation exceeded 25 percent of national income, inflationary pressures would follow. Maynard Keynes, to whom Dr. Clark wrote on the subject, answered that "as a practical proposition I should be strongly disposed to agree. . . ."[5] Since then, his

---

* With national production still increasing, the fact that the danger point had been passed was noticed at the time by only a small minority.

theory has received practical empirical backing, as democracies in which taxation exceeds 25 percent usually face economic pressure of increasing magnitude, in addition to varying degrees of inflation.

In spite of the multitude of literature on both public finance and futurology, and approved budgets for the subject, no system has since been devised to assess budgetary performance or standards of tax collection or to update these standards once every, say, three to five years.

HOW LARGE SHOULD THE INTERNAL REVENUE SYSTEM BE?

In a model state, in which voluntary self-assessment would be expected to be very close to complete, the Internal Revenue Service could be very small. It would justify its existence by carrying out random tax investigations; by collecting, recording, and confirming receipt of taxes; and by acting as a friendly adviser on pertinent matters to the citizen. Americans used to be proud of how small the number of Internal Revenue Service employees was. In comparison with other democracies, the yields of the American Internal Revenue Service were higher and their existence usually not very bothersome to the community in which they operated. As long as voluntary compliance was believed to be effective, embracing all but the outer reaches of society, the efficacy of the services was a point of pride with the U.S. administration. American, like British, Dutch, and, possibly, Scandinavian, income earners were believed to be honest taxpayers. So it was assumed that the size of the Internal Revenue Service could be kept small. But it does not appear to be that simple any longer.

Until the instruments with which to measure the size of the gross domestic product and gross national product are substantially changed and refined, it will remain difficult, probably impossible, even to try to assess how large tax enforcement systems should be. Or how effective it would be to, say, double the number of tax officers. Questions arise as to how multiplying the force would affect the country: Would it be a more pleasant place in which to live? What would be the cost in dollars of investing in doubling the force and what would be the social impact? What are the ancillary prerequisites of government that would convince society to increase its voluntary compliance? How should the subject be approached? Is it purely a technical matter of how to be more efficient or does it lead to more general questions concerning the quality of life and the degree of commitment of the individual to society?

Most democratic administrations have approached the subject totally unaware of the full size of the unmeasured economy. With little theoretical study or practical investigation, the subject is regarded as one that should be dealt with by the Internal Revenue Service itself. This is where the responsibility is generally thought to rest. To satisfy their curiosity and keep them abreast of the services rendered, politicians, in Congress or Parliament, should be submitted periodic reports by the tax commissioner and his or her staff. It is not to be expected that the legislators offer technical expertise as to how to manage or monitor the system.

HOW BIG IS THE SUBTERRANEAN ECONOMY?

Since early in 1979, senior executives in the accounting and tax branches of the civil service on both sides of the Atlantic have been involved in guessing the size of the unreported economy. Nobody knows for sure, but everybody has their own method of computing it. It is suspected but not proved that, in part, the revenue officers playing this game are trying either to shock their public and press for larger departmental budgets or, for other reasons, to play the phenomenon down, knowing well that nobody's guess is better than theirs.

In 1972, the American General Accounting Office[6] estimated that approximately 5 million people did not file tax returns (see also Chapter 11, pp. 114–115). The resultant tax debt was about $2 billion. Then, anticipating a congressional investigation that took place in 1979, the Internal Revenue Service prepared its own report, according to which $135 billion taxable income went unreported in 1976, with an ensuing loss of about $26 billion in revenue! Half to three-quarters of the unreported income came from legal sources; $25 billion was estimated to come from illegal sources. In the report, Internal Revenue Commissioner Jerome Kurtz pledges himself to intensify investigations. At the subsequent hearings, he repeated the pledge.

Then, in 1980, the same Commissioner Kurtz estimated that, since 1976, the subterranean economy had continued to grow and could have produced $300 billion by 1979 to 1980. Professor Alan J. Donziger expresses the belief that this economy could be as low as $200 billion, but he has also heard of figures reaching $700 billion.[7] The common denominator to all the theories is that no one really knows the size of the subterranean economy for sure. But the gut feeling is that the unmeasured economy is large and is increasing at a somewhat more rapid pace than the measured one.

If it is any consolation, the guestimates hazarded across the Atlantic, in the United Kingdom and western Europe, are no more precise.

THE CASE OF THE LEAKY BUCKET

The modern subterranean economy came into being the day direct taxation was first levied (or the day foreign currency controls were introduced). It reached its present size because modern governments ignored its existence.

There is no direct correlation between an increase or decrease in the marginal rates of direct taxation and the growth of the subterranean economy. There is a somewhat delayed rise when tax rates are increased, but it will not contract following a drop in tax rates. A major change in the rates accompanied by a comprehensive public relations campaign could have a direct influence, but has, to date, not been attempted. Generally, the unmeasured economy is a few steps behind the open economy, and it takes some time for it to be influenced by tax rate changes.

It has only in recent years begun to be realized, and only by some maverick economists, that a substantial proportion of the taxes raised goes back, in cash or kind, to the very same households from which it came. But, according to Arthur Seldon, Professor Milton Friedman has estimated that only about one-third of the billions of dollars spent on social welfare in the United States reaches lower-income earners and helps them cross the poverty line.[8] The other two-thirds, partly in the form of education, welfare, and other services, are, in fact, redistributed among the same middle class and richer taxpayers from whom they come. A classic example of red tape, bureaucratic wastage, and inefficiency which government has not yet accepted.

Some speak of the leaky bucket syndrome. This is a concept developed by the late Arthur M. Okun,[9] the eminent economist who, in effect, described bureaucratic inefficiency as a "leak." On the assumption that one of the main purposes of taxation is to transmit money from the rich to the poor, the question is how much of the funds out of the taxes raised are lost by government before they reach their destination. An indication of inefficiency would be if any particular bucket were shown to have a big hole, with government wasting a large part of the taxes. When the size of the leak increases and its spread becomes public knowledge, it causes disillusionment and encourages the taxpayer to search for ways to avoid paying taxes. The obvious indication of the leaky bucket syndrome is the fact that western welfare states have been spending an increasing part of their budgets on the overheads of services which have been growing only slowly or not at all.*

THE NEW PASSIVE RESISTER

Different imperfections of government influence the subterranean economy: an inflated administration; incompetence and inefficiency in the civil service; an unpopular ruler conspicuously wasting his nation's wealth; or a minority government with which a significant part of the taxpaying community finds it difficult to identify. Clumsy and redundant legislation acts as another incentive for the development of the subterranean economy. Many believe that government is the single major culprit and blame it for causing the increase of the subterranean economy. Modern administrations are accused not only of being too big, but of being insensitive to the social environment. Then there are those like Barbara Shenfield who say that

> Governments (themselves) . . . have undermined respect for Law . . . witness the "deeming clause" in tax law, whereby the State deems something to be what it is not, the very practice which in high dudgeon the State alleges against the tax evader and the lawful tax avoider . . . the "tax traps" in the wording of the law which catch the

* In the twenty years between 1960 and 1980, while the number of Americans increased by close to a quarter (23.3 percent), the federal budget increased by more than fivefold, increasing by 528 percent. Hardly any U.S. citizens believe that the quality of government, during these two decades, improved to a parallel degree.

innocent citizen, not because the legislature wished to tax him (it did not) but because it worded the law in such a way as to be construed against him by the Courts. . . .

And she concludes, "He who wishes to exorcise disrespect for the Law from our society, —should fix his eyes on the main culprits. The omnipotent, omnicompetent, high-taxing, high spending State is surely first among them."

And it is in this vein that D. R. Myddleton adds: "If Parliament allows the Government itself to override the Law, it is hypocrisy to object when citizens evade taxes."[10]

Although the tax criminal does not usually rationalize his evasion on the grounds of government incompetence, if the administration performed more effectively, the incidence of evasion might contract substantially. A relatively recent development is the arrival on the scene of the passive resister to the rules and regulations of the establishment, sometimes taking his or her economy underground. This citizen is disenchanted with officialdom and its ineptness, often angry at the abrasive manner of civil servants on all rungs of the establishment, jealous of the increasingly high salaries of some veteran bureaucrats and their attractive tax perks, and disgusted at the very light work burden of, for example, officials at the European Economic Community offices or other international institutions. The resister's appearance may be said to coincide with the other phenomena of modern society: permissiveness and anarchy.

THE MACROECONOMISTS' MEASUREMENTS ARE SUBSTANDARD

Any attempt to confront inflation, unemployment, or the structure of the budget of income and expenditure must include a discussion as to the best way of distributing the national pie through long-term economic planning, a reordering of priorities, and reorganizing the budget itself. And it must take the subterranean economy into account. An economy that produces black capital and evades taxes may, in the short run, prove to be more of a problem than the authorities have heretofore admitted. Its growth is increasingly felt even if present methodology by which the gross national product is measured may not be sophisticated enough to identify the full size of the subterranean economy.

In recent years, the credibility of the national economic indicators of various countries has been increasingly brought into question by some maverick economists who contend that the gross national product is really much larger than the officially published figures would indicate. The current method of assessing the gross national product, developed several decades ago, does not satisfactorily cover all the economic activities of any given nation today; larger and larger elements of production are escaping measurement by these macroeconomic instruments.

Gross national product accounts underreport or totally exclude many activities which would have a material effect on their figures, ranging from moonlighting and the illegal employment of aliens, covert rentals and barter, to certain business activities of the multinational groups which manage to escape detection. There are continuous new indications that the subterranean economy is growing faster than its overt counterpart, measured by government officials. The balance of economic resources is being shifted, none too slowly, toward the former.

The number of those convinced of the seriousness of the covert economy is obviously on the rise. Not all, however, even among the professional economists, are alive to its impact on the national accounts. They do not realize, for instance, that a series of misleading statistical figures results from the failure to recognize the subterranean economy. The full extent of the error is, for obvious reasons, not fully documented, but it has been pointed out[11] that the pace and level of inflation is overstated; price levels in the unreported economy are often lower than in the measured one. Artisans will usually lower their prices if they can provide their services without documenting them. Evading value-added tax (VAT) and, ultimately, income tax permits the producers to lower their prices and the consumers their costs. It has the unintentional effect of slowing down the inflationary spiral. This is certainly true where there is active competition between those practicing in the overt and covert economies, as in house repairs and maintenance.

If a significant part of those thought to be unemployed actually partake in the hidden economy and supply unmeasured commodities or services, then adding their contribution to the official gross national product figures would show that the national growth of the western countries is better than present calculations indicate. This is certainly evident in Italy, and probably so in the social welfare democracies.

There is much criticism of the horrendous modern bureaucracy. Had the correct measurement of labor been made and those operating in the hidden economy been included, the proportion of bureaucrats to the entire work force would be seen to be somewhat lower than thought at present. On consideration of these facts, to which must be added the unrecorded and untaxed income, it should be recognized that the average tax paid on the real gross national product is lower than indicated in official publications. *Time* says that the system has, at times, been "credited with contributing a dash of dynamism to the economy."[12]

The Economist first acknowledged the problem when it wrote that "adding up GNP by way of figures for spending now regularly produces a larger sum than the supposedly identical total reached by aggregating incomes: and for the self-employed, the gap between spending and declared income is particularly glaring. . . ."[13]

Academic and social research institutes give tenure to many thousand theoretical economists, and governments employ innumerable armies of statisticians to record, analyze, measure, and compare data. These institutions continue to use the information collected, ignoring the fact that it is quite evidently incomplete.

Planning the gross national product of any country and its pace of growth, its tolerable rate of inflation and unemployment; establishing a policy for incomes and wages—in all these functions politicians must take decisions on the basis of the data supplied by the statisticians. With the data in recent years becoming increasingly unreliable, it is little wonder that social welfare policies and gallant experiments such as that of British Prime Minister Mrs. Margaret Thatcher prove disappointing.[14]

However, the macrostatisticians and their economic counterparts have not yet seriously reexamined their techniques. They prefer to ignore the danger signals of their measuring instruments being no longer applicable. As long as the macroeconomists are not aware of the larger loopholes in their computations and do not warn their public, the politicians and the senior civil servants responsible for tax collection will try to disprove any claim that evasion is rampant. Thus, government macroeconomists inadvertently ally with their internal revenue colleagues in turning a blind eye to the subterranean economy.

REFERENCES

1. Theodore S. Lowi, "The Second Republic of the United States: The Permanent Receivership," in *The End of Liberalism 1978—Part IV Beyond Liberalism,* 2d ed., Norton, 1979.
2. "Make the Best of the Black Economy," *The Economist,* June 30, 1979.
3. Robert J. Samuelson, "Notes from the 'Underground Economy,'" *National Journal,* September 15, 1979.
4. "Public Expenditure in the U.K., Myth & Reality," *The Barclays Bank Review,* May 1980, pp. 33–37.
5. Colin Clark, "The Scope for, and Limits of, Taxation," in *The State of Taxation,* Readings of the Institute of Economic Affairs, No. 16, London, pp. 21–23.
6. Hearings before the Subcommittee on Oversight of the Committee on Ways and Means, House of Representatives, on the Underground Economy, July 16, 1979, Allen R. Voss, then Director, General Government Division, General Accounting Office.
7. In an interview with the *Philadelphia Enquirer,* "He's fathoming the underground economy's depth," June 16, 1980.
8. See Arthur Seldon, *Charge,* Temple Smith, London, 1977, p. 161.
9. Arthur M. Okun, *Equality and Efficiency: The Big Tradeoff,* Chapter 4, The Brookings Institute, Washington, D.C., 1977.
10. *Tax Avoision,* Reading No. 22 of the Institute for Economic Affairs, London, 1979, p. 45.
11. Vito Tanzi, "Underground Economy Built on Illicit Pursuits Is Growing Concern of Economic Policymakers," *International Monetary Fund Survey,* February 4, 1980.
12. *Time,* International Edition, December 1, 1980, p. 13.
13. "Make the Best of the Black Economy," *The Economist,* June 30, 1979, pp. 73–74.
14. See also Norris Willatt, "Europe's Moonlighting Millions," *Management Today,* July 1979, pp. 62–65.

5

INEPT GOVERNMENT AND INFLATION FEED THE SUBTERRANEAN ECONOMY

There was no profanity in the original languages of most American Indians. But of course, there was no federal income tax, either.

—FRANKLIN JONES

It is gradually dawning on politicians and economists that the way they have heretofore used the old monetary and fiscal instruments is no longer applicable. But why? The reasons include oversize government budgets and too little knowledge of the extent and range of operating funds, whether unmonitored or controlled, coming from both foreigners and the subterranean economy.

Why do the fiscal and monetary instruments developed since the end of World War II and apparently satisfactory during the following twenty-five years no longer perform adequately? In trying to answer this question, attention has been given to the petrocrisis and the increases in the cost of energy. The use of the term "stagflation" has become common, and many people have offered depressionary analyses pointing to the inevitability of it all. But there has not yet been any really satisfactory explanation of what has happened to the free economy.

During the 1970s, experts believed their countries could achieve prosperity through fine-tuning the economies; that is, they could achieve direct growth by increasing or decreasing the supply of money at varying interest percentages and by adjusting tax rates. By the end of the decade, they realized that they had failed and were perhaps at a dead end. There has been no satisfactory official explanation for this failure. Certainly, no one has conceded publicly that one reason was that the economists had underestimated the extent, growth, and power of the subterranean economy.

No one can state scientifically just how large the subterranean economy is. Research can prove it exists, describe its patterns of behavior, put forth reasons for its growth, explain at least part of its widening influence on society, and analyze the highlights of the interaction between the subterranean and the overt economy. But all that falls a considerable way short of drawing a detailed, comprehensive map of the subterranean economy. It remains elusive.

Official government pronouncements and policy have, so far, tended to ignore the presence of this economy. Most chiefs of internal revenue have paid little heed to its power. They took no serious steps to slow down the spread of the covert economy. In certain cases, they charged those who were warning of the phenomenon with dangerously encouraging it. In spite of the many indications that tax discipline has been declining, little has been done to stop the growth of evasion, even where it is most obvious. Pious public pronouncements about more vigorous steps of implementation, made by the heads of the various Ministries of Finance, and the conscientiousness of some of their staff have not been enough to improve the efficiency of the tax collection system.

POLITICIANS HAVE LOST CONTROL AND AVOISIONERS HAVE TAKEN OVER

It is questionable whether today's laws with very high marginal rates are such because the public wish it. While individuals may not want to pay taxes and think others should do it for them, that does not imply that most people understand the difference between a progressive, graduated tax and a proportional one. Walter J. Blum and Harry Kalven, Jr., say that most people cannot comprehend the implications of a progressive tax. They can grasp the idea that the rich should pay more tax than other classes, but not that the rich should pay a proportionately bigger tax.[1]

It is virtually impossible to measure what a fair redistribution of the tax burden would be. Myddleton observes that, while politicians are happy to expose consciences when opposing capital punishment, which is supposed to be supported by the public majority, they seem unwilling to adopt the same attitude when discussing progressive taxation.[2]

It is in this climate that tax avoision represents a possibility of preserving wealth and appears to be a sensible step in an era of high taxation, excessive inflation, and virtually stagnant growth in the official GNP. More and more honorable citizens of good tax standing and respectability are receiving unabashed, practical offers from artisans to carry out work for cash at what are obviously bargain prices as compared to the fee for the same job if recorded.

Together with more unrecorded cash services, barter has been rediscovered. Multibusiness barter exchanges are in operation in major areas from New York to Atlanta, Georgia and San Diego, California. They keep inventory records but not books of account. Members of these exchanges may bring in their products and draw from the stores of the exchange commodities to a value equal to the ones they have brought. On a more modest level, typical barter exchanges include those between physician and electrician, lawyer and architect, restaurateur and advertising agency, and so on.

Cash, barter, banking services, and overseas financial outlets are the more common instruments used by members of the underground economy, in that descending order of prevalence.

The larger the unmeasured economy, the less precise the official statistics of the GNP and the other national accounts. One of the bases, for instance, on which the GNP is calculated and which is suspected of being inaccurately presented since the late 1970s is the official unemployment statistics. Are these exaggerated and overestimated, acting as a stimulant to policymakers to provide additional positions, thus heating the economy and contributing to inflation? If, indeed, a fair or substantial proportion of the average 5 to 8 percent officially unemployed in the United States, the United Kingdom, and other western democracies are, in fact, gainfully occupied off the record, two sets of economic assumptions might prove to be wrong: the first relates to the extent of economic stagnation or recession, and the second deals with the generally accepted reasons why the stabilizing elements introduced to lessen unemployment are not more effective.[3]

This explains, in part, the increasing government failure to fine tune its monetary and fiscal policies. For a substantial part of earnings, capital, and cash flow outside the sphere of direct regulatory influence, such administrative instruments are hardly applicable.

The American recession that began late in 1979 was six months later than the projections of reputable economists. One explanation put forward was that people, in fact, have more money than the economists realize; that they sensibly juggle their funds (not only their books) and can thus put off the economic embarrassment, insolvency, or bankruptcy predicted by the theorists.[4]

One of the complaints commonly heard is that it is the law-abiding citizen who pays for the sins of the income tax evader: to make up for his or her default, the honest taxpayer must pay a higher rate of taxes. Any disinterested observer of the way bureaucracy works should be highly skeptical of a claim that if government collected, say, 15 percent more income than before it would reduce taxes correspondingly. Attempts to limit government spending to a prearranged figure have not proven successful. Governments collect all the taxes they can and will always find uses for any extra funds they manage to bring in.

The sad thing about the tax system is that, as the rates began to rise and the number of people with taxable incomes became overwhelming, the politicians responsible for the legislation and the tax specialists with whom they consulted were mostly interested in raising the money required by the increasingly inflexible government expenditure machine. They were not aware of the social ramifications of turning the entire population into potential taxpayers or the impact of allowing their tax agents to require individuals to present documentation of their financial activities—which many, today, regard as an invasion of privacy.

BIG GOVERNMENT MEANS A BIG SUBTERRANEAN ECONOMY

It is believed by those who know that in the totalitarian and authoritarian states the number and percentage of people who partake in illegal economic activity is probably considerable. Similarly, one can probably say that the larger the public budget, the more income is likely to go unreported. At a certain point, already reached in most democracies, administrations committed to spend more and more money on public finance upset the delicate moral balance of the population. As a result of large government, the number of lawbreakers in the western open society is well in the tens and possibly even in the hundreds of millions. It is still far from known to what extent the trend to disregard the laws of the land has led to a lower level of identification with one's country or to poorer national motivation.

The direct administrative costs of government and the increased amounts of transfer payments, including those for old-age pensioners, welfare recipients, social services, education, and so on, all accelerate the subterranean economy. Government expenditures both for bureaucracy and for transfer payments have been growing in size, becoming more cumbersome and less popular over recent years. As criticism of the various elements of expenditure in the budget has increased, the attractions of joining the unmeasured economy have grown, combined with a disappearing fear of getting caught, which is supported by the general belief in government incompetence. There used to be a consensus among the respectable bourgeoisie that not declaring taxable income was risky. Hesitancy to go underground stemmed not only from the danger of being fined heavily or sent to jail, but also from the risk of being cast out socially, of being turned into a pariah after the legal penalty had been paid. Society would bar ex-tax convicts from the social and economic positions occupied before their "fall." Nowadays, there is little loss of face on being caught. Tax evaders may not be invited to meet the Queen, but they will certainly not be blackballed by their clubs. They will probably be regarded as having had a spot of bad luck. Their colleagues, whether avoiders themselves or perfectly law-abiding citizens, will sympathize and encourage them in their adversity.

The increasing disenchantment of the public with big government is in a way paradoxical. While, in many ways, the individual's dependence on the state has grown—from free schooling and medication through old-age pensions—there is far more criticism of the hand that feeds. There is less of a spirit of dedication to or cooperation with one's country. In the nineteenth century, there was incomparably more identification with the Fatherland. At that time, taxes and the total government budget averaged less than 5 percent of the GNP. There was no difficulty calling young able-bodied men to arms for World War I or II; the number of conscientious objectors was insignificant. Now, all over the free society there are increasing doubts; if and when today's young people are called to the flag, it is not at all clear that draft and recruiting avoidance will not be a serious social and security problem. There were certainly worrying signs in the avoidance of the draft law in the United States until it ended in the early 1970s and in the resistance expressed in 1980 to the reintroduction of the draft.

While draft avoidance is visible, joining the subterranean economy is (by definition) much less so. Still, to a large extent, it expresses a similar protest. One avoider argues, "Your security priorities are not mine"; the other, "Your social expenditure programs are not mine." Because draft resistance is so much more open, government is more sensitive to it than to the grayer realm of the unmeasured economy. As an open issue it is freely discussed, and a party fighting an election must take a stand on the question.

The subterranean economy is of a more complicated nature. Although a few have rationalized its existence and turned it into an ideology which they are willing to present in public, most of its practitioners would not stand up to be counted. It is almost as if there is collusion between them and the rest of society, each for their own reasons, to keep a low profile. Why the members of the subterranean economy prefer not to publicize their legitimate avoidance schemes or their less clearly legal evasion is understandable. The reason why the treasuries and the politicians do not take stronger action to prevent them or, at least, to reduce the extent of underground activities is less understandable.

The majority of civil servants do not as yet address themselves to the existence of the subterranean economy, and those who do recognize it are content to take no action. They argue that, by increasing exposure of the unmeasured activity, they will only whet the appetites of some of the law-abiding, taxpaying community, who will then decide to cross into the covert economy. Thus, the argument runs, the state stands to lose by the greater publicity, rather than to gain.

THE TAX MACHINE SUDDENLY MUSHROOMED

In 1979, some 90 million tax returns were filed with the Internal Revenue Service.* Income tax is probably the law that most directly affects the largest number of individuals in the United States. And yet, the history of direct taxation in the United States is briefer than that of the United Kingdom—just over a century old. We see from *The Federal Income Tax* (p. 89) that Mark Twain was delighted when he paid his first income taxes in 1864 for a total, including fines, of $36.82. The payment made him feel "important"! In 1872, income tax was repealed, only to be reenacted into law in 1894, when President Cleveland was convinced that the then basis for collecting revenue was obsolete and drew too little money from the professional and business worlds. However, he heard some strong words against his bill; Senator John Sherman of Ohio, of the Sherman Antitrust Act, decried it for smacking of socialism and communism; a congressman opposed it for being too inquisitorial, morally distasteful, and impractical, necessitating an army of officials to enforce it.

By 1913, Congress had enacted a law for a graduated tax on individuals, ranging from 1 to 7 percent, and a flat 1 percent tax rate on the net profits of corporations. Since then, the history of taxation in the United States has been that of rising rates and special alleviating provisions to save people in the upper brackets from the inconveniences of having to pay taxes.

To make matters more difficult, the tax laws use complicated, verbose language that can easily depress the reader willing to attempt to surmount its heights. From its virtually insignificant size before World War II, the basic statute—the code—grew to be approximately 1200 pages long in 1980. There are 3000 pages of treasury regulations, and the formidable Federal Tax Case Law requires fifty feet of shelf space. The definition, for example, of the word "employment" comprises more than a thousand words, nineteen semicolons, and forty-two simple parentheses.[5]

There are other examples of how almost totally incoherent the Code has become. Some of the sentences are so long, it is difficult to decipher their meaning. There is, for instance, one

---

* Compared to the 84 million who voted in the November 1980 U.S. presidential elections.

sentence 379 words long (Section 170(b)(i)(A)); another of 385 words (Section 6651 (a)); and one reaching 506 words (Section 7701(a)(19))! Others may be shorter but are virtually impossible to follow, such as the last sentence of Section 509(a), which reads:

For purposes of paragraph (3), an organization described in Paragraph (2) shall be deemed to include an organization described in Section 501(c)(4), (5) or (6) which would be described in Paragraph (2) if it were an organization described in Section 501(c)(3).

Irving Younger, in his article "Socrates and US," published in *Commentary* for December 1980, envisions the day when a judgment of the U.S. courts will be given declaring the Internal Revenue Code unconstitutional, based on the argument that (1) the plaintiff does not understand it, (2) nobody understands it, and (3) it is therefore invalid. With all the staff in their employ, congresspersons who legislate such objectionable non-English have little justification for infuriating Americans out of the tax system. The average American has no way of seriously understanding the code's contents, and it is one that no citizen can comply with unaided. There is an awareness of the need to stop this kind of verbosity. Eight states, including New York, New Jersey, Connecticut, Maine, and Hawaii have passed comprehensive "plain-English" laws. Minnesota, Wisconsin, and Ohio have laws on their books about the wording of insurance policies. The Connecticut statute forbids sentences longer than an average of twenty-two words; no single sentence may be longer than fifty words.* Should one be encouraged by such laws or depressed?

TAXES JUST GREW

Until World War II, direct taxes were not a (very) heavy burden on democratic society. The majority of the population was not affected by income tax laws; the rates were moderate and applied only to the upper-middle classes and the wealthier elements of society. Tax ordinances were relatively simple and it was believed, in the English-speaking world at least, that they were applied quite effectively. Public opinion in the United States and the United Kingdom was that if any tax

---

* *Journal of Accountancy,* July 1981, p. 135.

evaders existed they should be sought out, brought to trial, and sentenced as required by law.

Some future macroeconomists and tax historians, describing the growth of capitalism up to the advent of World War II, may possibly refer to that period as the "Age of Tax Innocence."

Tax rates were raised substantially for the duration of both World Wars. Both times the move was understood by the majority and accepted as a wartime necessity. In those periods of patriotic enthusiasm and identification with the state, civilians were expected to do everything they could for the "cause"—including the payment of all taxes. There were always the war profiteers and those who tried to escape the network, but they were regarded as scum and, when caught, punished by the courts with full popular approval.

After World War II, taxes were not substantially reduced. For the first time, marginal peacetime tax rates, even for the middle classes and corporate business, exceeded 40 and often 50 percent. In the United Kingdom, the Scandinavian countries, and several others, they reached well over 85 percent. The moderately wealthy discovered that, on part of their income, they were being taxed at more than 90 percent! At first, some did not fully realize the social changes these taxes meant. Optimists among both governors and governed believed that these high rates were still temporary measures, to remain in force until postwar economic and social normalization was attained. But, by the end of the 1950s, when neither the Republican administration of President Eisenhower nor Prime Minister Macmillan's Conservative government had reduced tax rates, it became clear that income taxes for the middle classes were here to stay. Government had become a much larger establishment than ever before and its ever-increasing expenditure required continuously larger revenue.

There was a certain acceptance of the system as unquestionable and inevitable. From the start, few people really believed tax rates would be cut or planned for such an eventuality. Some among those, still the majority, who wished to remain within the establishment were encouraged when a new business term sprung up: tax planning (a euphemism for tax avoidance). A new profession appeared—that of the tax consultant. But others more discreetly began thinking about moving out and into the subterranean economy.

Many Americans decided simply to ignore the existence of income tax. Few believed they were risking much. After all, the Internal Revenue staff, dependent on compliance, always limited in size, can only audit a small number of the population. Some of those audited are law-abiding citizens. The authorities may have their doubts about others.

When such doubts are supported by documentation, an investigation may be opened. Fraud litigation, however, is rare. The number of court cases is insignificant, by any count. The specialists explain this by the inefficiency of the overextended tax inspectors, who prefer the easier job of collecting taxes from the measured economy to attempting to root out the undeclared funds. Even when strong suspicion arises that unmeasured income exists, preparing an evasion case that will stick requires much time-consuming research, effort, and energy. It is often simpler, cheaper, and more effective to settle out of court. From close to 90 million people who filed income tax returns and the many millions more who should have but did not, the American federal authorities commenced proceedings in connection with tax evasion against nearly 10 thousand in the six years from 1975 to 1980. Some 3600 were convicted and sent to prison for an average sentence of seventeen months. In 1980 alone, 1832 proceedings were begun, with 740 jail sentences being handed down.*

The Canadians are even more liberal in their approach. In the year that ended June 30, 1980, the total number of prosecutions under Section 238 of the Income Tax Act reached 9001. The eight(!) who were convicted and the nine convicted under Section 239 all received jail sentences of fourteen days to two years.

Figures for Britain are not more dissuading. In 1978, a total of ninety-nine people were prosecuted for offenses connected with taxation, of whom a quarter were sent to prison. Fifty more were prosecuted the next year and twenty-five imprisoned. For 1980, the figure was 149, with 14 jailed.

---

* The number of criminal proceedings and convictions in the United States since the mid-1970s in connection with tax evasion is:

	1975	1976	1977	1978	1979	1980
Criminal proceedings	1495	1331	1636	1724	1820	1832
Jail sentences	485	486	685	681	675	740

In other countries in the West, total numbers were generally as insignificant. The number of those, for instance, against whom legal proceedings for direct tax evasion were instituted in the Netherlands in 1977 was ninety-one. More ambitious, and covering indirect taxes as well, were the Swedes, who charged 1568 people in 1979 and imprisoned 826. A similar number of proceedings was instituted in France.

Quite clearly, there is no relationship between the minimal number of those practicing evasion recognized by the government and the attempt, let alone the effectiveness, of the administration to deter them. Chances of being caught and imprisoned are usually less than those of being involved in a traffic accident and physically less punishing.

VALUES ARE CHANGING

Few realized that, even among the members of the open economy, doubts were developing about payment morality. Little publicity, for instance, was given to a 1975 U.S. survey which revealed that, of the 531 top managers questioned, 48 percent said they would practice bribery if it were prevalent in the foreign country in which they were working. A fair number of them felt pressured to compromise on personal ethics for the sake of corporate goals.[6]

In a period of unabating inflation, itself a result of weak economic policies and unsatisfactory leadership, a situation arises of conflicting interests between the individual and the state. There is empirical evidence among those studying the subject that says the higher the inflation, the greater the economic uncertainty; and it follows that, in periods of inflation, confidence in the efficiency of government becomes weaker and social insecurity more marked.[7] As a consequence, new values come to the fore to justify one's struggle for survival in an increasingly hostile environment.

Thus, the subterranean economy grows parallel to inflation. Modern tax dodgers are often in other respects law-abiding citizens, earning their living ethically and honorably. They believe they have some sort of moral justification in protecting their families and themselves by opting for the subterranean economy.

REFERENCES

1. Walter J. Blum and Harry Kalven, Jr., *The Uneasy Case for Progressive Taxation,* Chicago, 1953, p. x.
2. D. R. Myddleton, *Tax Avoision,* IEA Readings No. 22, London, 1979, p. 4.
3. Professor Edgar L. Feige makes similar comments in "How Big Is the Irregular Economy?" *Challenge,* November/December 1979, pp. 5–13.
4. See also Donald Bauder, "Underground Economy, Life Without the IRS," *Las Vegas Sun,* March 11, 1979.
5. Internal Revenue Code, 1980.
6. See also Donald R. Cressy, "The Roots of Management Fraud: A Case of Multiple Moralities," *World,* Spring 1980.
7. F. Harvey Popell writes on this subject in "How Inflation Undermines Morality," *Business Week,* May 5, 1980, p. 20.

6

TAXMANSHIP—AVOIDANCE OR EVASION

Avoidance or evasion—away from morality and into gamesmanship? How else to describe the double standard approach to tax collecting? Certainly, the enormous fund of energy and expertise spent by consultants, bankers, and professionals has been worldwide. To make it more "interesting," the rules of the game change, even more than in other sports. If the commissioner of Internal Revenue in the United States can convince the administration and then Congress or if the chancellor of the exchequer disagrees with a high court decision, they will propose a tax amendment in the next budget. One is reminded of Alice's bewilderment when she went through the looking glass: "That's not a regular rule; you have invented it just now." "It's the oldest rule in the book," said the King. "Then it ought to be Number One," said Alice.

In official jargon, tax avoidance is lawful, tax evasion unlawful. In avoidance, the taxpayer, knowing what the tax is, chooses not to expose him- or herself to illegal activities. In evasion, the same taxpayer risks making him- or herself liable for tax if caught, and chooses to conceal this liability from the authorities. When, years ago, life was more simple and innocent, no one thought there was anything immoral or unpatriotic about tax avoidance. Indeed, reading about the tax morality of up to less than a generation ago, one might think that tax paying took the form of the game of "How to Succeed in Avoidance Without Really Evading." American, British, and other English-speaking courts of today still interpret literally Judge Learned Hand's finding of 1934 that "anyone may so arrange his affairs that his taxes shall be as low as possible: he is not bound to choose that pattern which best pays the Treasury. Everyone does it, rich and poor alike, and all do right; for nobody owes any public duty to pay more than the law demands."

More people than ever are interpreting his opinion imaginatively and still more will do so.

ON RETROACTIVE TAX LEGISLATION

One of the most demoralizing and discouraging instruments of government is the use of retroactive or retrospective legislation.

Not all governments have developed this habit, certainly not continuously. But retroactive legislation does occur even in democracies, and is usually related to changes in the tax laws. D. R. Myddleton says that "there is no difference in principle between taxing people on income which was not legally taxable at the time it arose (or at rates higher than those in force at the time) and punishing them for 'offenses,' such as trading with a future enemy, for example, which were not legally offenses at the time they were committed (or increasing the penalties after the event."[1] There are those who claim that legislation is not really retroactive if it carries the change in law back to the day when government first announced its intention to enact that law. This leads to an interesting and novel twist which may be termed "the rule of the threat of law"; the rule of arbitrary political opinion according to which taxpayers stand to suffer if they ignore the warning but have no redress if they heed it and government then decides to change its tax plans.

Making penal laws effective before their enactment means that nobody can ever know where he or she stands or be sure that his or her actions will not, in hindsight, be regarded as illegal. Myddleton concludes that "preventing citizens from knowing the law is like Caligula's practice of posting tax laws in an awkwardly cramped spot and written so small that no one could copy."[2]

AVOISON IS IN

Ours is an economy that encompasses both tax evasion and avoidance. The British Institute of Economic Affairs put out, in 1979, a Special Reading on the subject, in which it attempted to describe the economic, legal, and moral interrelationship between avoidance and evasion. In it, Arthur Seldon, editorial director of the Institute, defined tax avoision as the moral blurring of the legal distinction between avoidance and evasion arising from the rejection of high and arbitrary taxation. In his prologue to the papers presented in the Special Reading, he warns that avoision should not be crushed at all costs because its suppression might cause a greater loss in national income than the political benefits derived from maintaining an otherwise questionable policy.[3] Indeed, this proposition is becoming accepted by more and more economists.

The Laffer curve, first drawn by Professor Arthur Laffer of the University of Southern California, illustrates a basically similar claim: tax rates are subject to a law of diminishing returns. Beyond an optimum tax rate, aggregate tax collections will actually drop.

Avoision includes all actions, legal or otherwise, that reduce tax payments. Emigrating to a Caribbean tax haven to save income taxes and death duties, even though the new country offers a better climate and a more peaceful way of life, is legal avoision. It is proposed to state unequivocally that as long as taxes are imposed, avoision cannot be suppressed.

Income tax was originally designed to tax the well-to-do and that at a moderate rate. It was never meant to raise taxes from the general public. Many of its ills result from this misconception and the fact that in the past generation it has been applied wrongly.

Avoidance is an amoral pastime that was encouraged in an age when form was more important than content. In the last third of the twentieth century, however, the approach to life has changed materially. Emphasis today is on substance; form takes second place.

The blindness of the legislatures throughout the democracies has been and still is that they believe they can turn all the wage- and capital-earning population into full taxpayers. At no point in history could this be done.

Tax systems with high rates seemed to work well until recently, not least because of the loopholes offered to mitigate their impact. Wealthy Americans still recall with nostalgia how, until the late 1950s, capital gains tax provided them with a delightful vehicle through which to avoid high rates on personal income. Tax shelters were popular in the past decade; then the administration attempted to curb their use. Antiavoidance legislation seems to be part of the game and is a favorite pastime of legislatures but, while it is true that some gaps were overexploited, most updated corrective acts have inherent in them potential that supplies the creative and imaginative tax consultant with any number of new loopholes.

The internal revenue services of various countries were encouraged by the politicians to turn a blind eye to the growing amounts of invisible income, and thus the system of perks, another unmeasured field, flourished. Perks include all the bonuses and fringe benefits that a large number of employees all over the world receive but which are not assessed as part of their take-home pay. They range from subsidized staff canteens for both blue- and white-collar workers through "representative clothing allowances" and the use of company vehicles, to free or almost-free airplane tickets for the employees of air carriers and tourist agencies. For some, the notional tax grossed up perks add up to a major part of their income.

It is, as yet, not accepted by government that it is impossible to maintain a dynamic, totally fair and equitable tax law at the prevailing welfare-state tax rates that will apply to the whole population.

Some believe that evasion is even larger than avoidance. Avoidance schemes are for the wealthy. They usually cost money in the form of professional fees and other charges, which they consider better invested than it would be if used to pay taxes. For them, an optimum reduction in tax rates may prove to be sufficiently attractive to persuade them to drop the schemes they have heretofore chosen. For the masses who opt for the subterranean economy and choose the path of evasion, the situation is different. They will not willingly agree to pay any tax. They never did, but, until the advent of World War II, the vast majority of the working population was not liable for income tax. The *highest* tax rates then were usually lower than the present *average* minimum of close to 25 percent.[4]

Neither tax avoidance nor evasion are recorded in the official national accounts of income, expenditure, or output of virtually all the democracies.

FROM EVASION THROUGH EXPENSE ACCOUNTS

It may be opportune at this point to cite examples of petty evasion. They probably start with moonlighting and the suburban artisan. Then there are the shopkeepers and licensees who can, for instance, pocket cash from the till; casual earnings which go unreported; personal expenses which are claimed as business outlays; petty smuggling; capital gains which are omitted; the personal belongings of a deceased relative which are not declared, and so on.

From this beginning, the subterranean economy took a qualitative leap forward when some of its practitioners chose, rather than just be consumers, to reinvest at least part of their proceeds in an unrecorded, productive, vertical business. The growth of this economy was made easier by the increased presence and power of other illegal capital, derived from a wide range of criminal activities, from protection and extortion money all the way to slush funds, bribery, and kickbacks.

The blue-collar moonlighter and the illegal *gastarbeiter* simply ignore the authorities and hope for the best. But when very substantial amounts of capital are involved, business magnates retain the services of tax consultants and benefit from their sometimes brilliant, if devious, evasion schemes.

While the American government has done a commendable job in introducing legislation (such as the Foreign Corrupt Practices Act of 1977) and in enforcing laws to reduce the frequency of bribery, kickbacks, and other forms of illegal payment in U.S. financial activities, it has been less successful in its efforts than official publications would have us believe. There are signs that foreign elements, often connected with petrofunds, are intent on circumventing these laws. In all other democracies, supercommissions, called by whatever name you will and recorded only in part if at all, are accepted as a necessary evil by both governments and most businessmen. These funds are often laundered and may remain invested in the local subterranean economy as a nest egg, growing steadily in net worth.

And then there are the expense accounts. It is not rare for one financial tycoon to invite another business czar for a working vacation aboard his yacht, hopping the Greek Islands. The czar will reciprocate by having the tycoon over at his retreat in the Colorado Rockies. It is more rare for them to arrange a "study tour" together, to evaluate, say, business conditions in the Bahamas, as James de Blueson,* a true blue-blooded Englishman, and Ernest van Redhorn, the aggressive hustler, did. At the end of their stay at the luxury island hotel, each loudly insisted on covering the other's hotel bill. Their joint lawyer, present at the time, later said he will never understand them, as each knew the other would claim the cost of the bill as a deductible expense, so that it was peanuts for either of them. But for the dozen or so onlookers in the hotel lobby, the scene was glamorous; they could not have imagined charging such an expensive vacation and then having the audacity to claim it as a tax deduction.

Treasury officials may disapprove in principle of many of the charges expensed in big corporations, but as long as the latter do not overstep the usually very liberal mark, the civil servants will rarely interfere. Executive salaries are expected to be high; executive amenities are rarely checked in depth in an official IRS audit. In this age of inflation and multibillion-dollar turnover, the inspectors usually prefer discretion to inquiry, even when they detect a gift worth, say, $25,000 given to a chief executive on some anniversary.

Expense accounts can become fanciful . . .

FROM AVOIDANCE TO EVASION

In many countries, including those which were, until recently, regarded as law abiding, income tax evasion has become part of the accepted mores, even among some of the political elite. There are considerable numbers of circles which no longer disapprove of the convicted tax criminal. Quite the contrary—sympathy is often shown to those few "unfortunate" evaders caught by the authorities; gone is the era in which respect or admiration was the reward of those who paid their taxes down to the last penny.

---

* Connie and I witnessed this, but the names and the locality are a figment of my imagination.

Consequently, the work of the tax collector has become far more difficult. This is especially noticeable in the advanced welfare states, which levy high direct taxes to finance their budgets.

In the United States, the United Kingdom, Scandinavia and the Benelux countries, and other democracies, people are amassing untaxed but taxable income with some degree of social acceptance, though most are not very ostentatious about it. Still, among the different indications of the arrival of the subterranean economy in the United States are the daily advertisements in the major dailies such as *The New York Times* and *The Wall Street Journal,* offering coin and stamp collections for sale at bargain prices against cash!

Income taxes are not the only consideration influencing the rising tide of participation in the subterranean economy. The cost of both the aggregate of all the various taxes payable and the time and money needed to do so is a major encouragement to opt out of the overt economy. Thus, for example, in all Common Market countries and others, dodging value-added tax is both usual and worthwhile. The same applies to national insurance, taxes designed to comply with minimum wage laws, and other employee protection measures both in western Europe and in North America.

The rich have a better deal and a sharper lawyer, and avoid. The "lower" middle classes, the white- and blue-collar workers, prefer to evade and save on their overhead. Not for them the sophistries of distinction between avoidance and evasion. Both groups are displaying greed for money and, at the same time, expressing disenchantment with government.

If the subterranean economy continues to increase in size, it cannot be disregarded and will not be made to go away by more effective policing alone. Its power, revealed by the fact that in all free countries it has, by now, the active cooperation of a significant part of the population, poses a much greater threat to government than the politicians realize.* No

* There are politicians who give public recognition to its existence. For instance, John Biffen, chief secretary to the British Treasury, acknowledged in the debate that took place in June 1979 on the budget that it was not known how much revenue was lost by moonlighting, but that there was a substantial problem with the black economy. See *The Guardian* of June 28, 1979.

democracy has long survived as such when a majority of its citizens regarded its institutions with mistrust.

Modern government, growing rigid in its habits and incapable, until now, at any rate, of reassessing its way of operation, is facing a serious, active vote of no confidence from both the active participants and the passive collaborators in the unmeasured economy.

It is felt that billions of what should be tax dollars are simply going into other people's pockets, so what harm can it do if one more member of the subterranean economy adds his or her mite to the pile?

The decision to opt out of the official economy is conscious only in part, but the result is the pasting together of a very significant proportion of the population into a front against the government. The abuse of the tax laws, first legally, against the imperial bureaucracy of government, then illegally, through tax evasion, is a direct result of the spreading distrust of the political and economic judgment of the party in power. People do not believe in the ability of the administration to spend the taxes on their hard-earned income efficiently and thriftily. Law-abiding, taxpaying citizens, avoiders and evaders alike, all have increasing doubts as to whether the various administrations are, in fact, spending "their" incomes better and putting the funds to wiser use than they would themselves. Government officials seem not sufficiently sensitive to these feelings of resentment and, if some are aware of the need to show the public an improved return on each dollar spent, they have not done so. They have not developed any reliable way of measuring the effectiveness of their services and plans, nor have they attempted to show that their programs are cost effective or that they themselves are seriously cost-minded. There is no evidence that they have thought of a possible alternative, such as a moderate tax rate, applying fairly and only to income earners in the upper brackets, which might prove to be a success if imposed by a government with effective, efficient, and generally popular policies.

DOES AVOISION CAUSE LOSSES TO THE FISC?

There has not, to date, been sufficient study of the nature of the subterranean economy. Nor has enough thought been given to the extent of the loss to the tax authorities resulting from avoidance and evasion. There is no doubt that, in the short term, taxes on income which remain unpaid are lost to the fiscal authorities; but if we analyze what happens in the long term we must distinguish between two main types of avoidance. There are those who feel that marginal tax rates are so high that it is better to reduce one's taxable work load and spend more time on one's hobbies or other forms of relaxation. They avoid taxation at the cost of income and may decide to repair their home in their spare time, rather than call in the carpenter or plumber, and save in expenditure in this and related ways. Other tax avoiders, contemplating new enterprises, may decide to save taxes by adopting tax-saving schemes. They are contributing to the gross national product and creating more taxable income at the same time as they are saving as much tax as possible.

Waiving potential income, reducing the amount of cash at one's disposal, and generating lower returns to the internal revenue service are all immediate and final. But avoidance together with self-enrichment, as in the second case, should, in the longer term, yield gains to others and, ultimately, to the authorities.

High tax rates tend to act as a disincentive to profitable production. Avoidance schemes and evasive tactics develop more rapidly, the more prohibitive tax rates are. An effective campaign would not coopt avoisioners into the fully taxed community, but might deter them from further activities. At the present level of official enthusiasm and efficiency, however, the likelihood of an effective campaign is more than remote—it is hypothetical.[5]

REFERENCES

1. See D. R. Myddleton, "Tax Avoision, Its Costs and Benefits," in *Tax Avoision,* IEA Readings No. 22, 1979, pp. 44–45.

2. Ibid.

3. "Tax Avoision," *Special Reading No. 22* of the Institute of Economic Affairs, London, 1979.

4. See also A. R. Ilersic, "The Economics of Avoidance/Evasion," in *Tax Avoision,* IEA Readings No. 22, London, 1979, pp. 23–40.

5. See also Barry Bracewell-Milnes, "The State of Taxation, the Fisc

and the Fugitive," *Special Reading No. 16* of the Institute of Economic Affairs, London, 1979, pp. 79–87.

7

WHO USES CASH AND BARTER?

One of the easiest, best-known, and safest methods of evasion is the use of cash. Cash income is common among moonlighters, artisans and artists, small businesspeople, and other petty evaders. All measurements carried out in the 1960s and 1970s show that, in spite of the advent of the most sophisticated, virtually instant electronic banking facilities, in many ways more convenient than any method of business transaction we have ever known, the growth in the use of cash is more rapid than that in the use of banking services.

In the simpler past, it was assumed that black money was kept in the form of cash; that it was too risky to record it or transmit it through banks. Professor Peter Gutman of Bernard M. Baruch College of the City University of New York, who is believed to have coined the phrase "subterranean economy" (see Chapter 1, footnote 1), proposed measuring the subterranean economy by the proportion of the growth of cash activity compared to demand deposits in banks. According to him, the amount of currency in circulation has been increasing faster than the value of demand bank deposits. He attributes this relatively faster growth to the continuous rise in the officially unmeasured economy.

It is still difficult to assess the effect of this cash economy on the real gross national product, but indications of its positive contributions are many—from anecdotal evidence of the Italian economic miracle through figures for some of the officially depressed areas of the United Kingdom. Lord Sieff of Marks & Spencer describes how he

> found that branches with the best sales of some high price commodities were not only in areas with high official employment . . . but also in areas with high unofficial employment . . . or high official unemployment but with social benefits supplemented by earnings from unofficial employment. Shrimps at £4 per pound were selling well in Cumberland, Lancashire, Newcastle and Plymouth, despite high official unemployment. I wondered why our business was buoyant in these areas . . . the conclusion I came to was that there is a bigger sub-economy in Britain than I ever dreamed of.[1]

MOONLIGHTING FOR CASH INCOME

The uninitiated should not be misled by the term "moonlighting." Not much of this work is carried out at night. It is a term that came into English from the United States and covers any kind of extra employment over and above one's basic job for which one gets paid. It may be undeclared work carried out by those officially regarded as unemployed or that second job which is not disclosed in the income tax returns. Among professionals in the United Kingdom, many prefer to call what they do a form of "free lancing," rather than "moonlighting."[2]

Moonlighters receive most of their pay in cash.

There are many who declare a substantial part of their income and pay taxes thereon but maintain an additional source of income on the side, hidden from the prying eyes of the treasury. Some are independent entrepreneurs, others employees whose income from a second job is kept out of sight.

The French are veteran moonlighters. The "chain of complicity" which links consumers wanting a job done fast and red tape cut with *le travail noir*[3] has reached such proportions that the government is worried. Some bureaucrats in France suspect that in 1980 the taxes evaded by moonlighters may have equalled billions of dollars! No wonder some French economists believe that at least several million workers are involved in moonlighting in their country.

There is an inherently cynical approach to the tax system in France, which is generally thought to accord many more benefits to the rich than to the proletariat. There is, therefore, an almost automatic sympathy for *le travail noir,* and those who practice it are respected for wishing to improve their standard of living.

French moonlighting began with various types of home repair and maintenance, such as plumbing jobs, but it has spread to cover all types of repair including automobile and electronic work, and personal services ranging from hairdressing to dressmaking. As in the United States, civil servants, including members of the police, are an important source of this unmeasured labor force.

Not only may your house painter and family doctor be adept tax evaders, but also famous film directors, like Ingmar Bergman, and the young sculptress in Denmark. She supported what was until 1979 her country's second largest political party, of which the main platform was how to do away with taxes. Progress party leader Mogens Glistrup, a tax lawyer by profession, proudly publicly claims he practices avoision constantly and encourages others to do the same.

There are other compelling reasons for some to evade income tax and social security charges. Many laborers from North Africa and southeast Europe working in western Europe are illegal *gastarbeiter,* with no work permit. There are also illegal Mexican and Puerto Rican immigrants in parts of the United States.* They are often willing to take cutthroat wages, preferably cash, if possible untraceable, as long as they can get work. Nobody knows their exact number, but the guesstimates range from a low of 5 million to 8 and 10 million in western Europe. As they are gradually absorbed into the U.S. economy, when they first arrive they are willing to take untaxed jobs at $.50 per hour, well below the legal minimum wage.

Until the economic recession in the late 1970s reduced demand, the number of *gastarbeiter* was increasing steadily. Their inability to get work permits has pushed them into the double role of producer and consumer in the subterranean economy. Attracted

---

* It is of interest to note that they are becoming entrepreneurial. In *The Economist* for December 27, 1970, Norman Macrae, the paper's deputy editor, quotes a Carter aide as having said that partly because of these people, "Nobody knows how big the unobserved economy is. There are some people who say it is as much as one-fifth or one-fourth of the size of the economy. . . ."

by their nonunion capacity for hard work at low cost, employers are willing to risk becoming party to the black economy by making use of their services.

The most striking change in moonlighting during the 1970s was in the proportion of women moonlighters. In the United States, about three out of every ten holders of multiple jobs in 1979 were women, nearly double the 16 percent of ten years earlier. According to a report on the subject,* most women moonlighters belong to the professional and technical groups, including schoolteachers and health workers. It used to be that the married man with two children was most likely to have a second job, but in the decade under review the proportion of married women moonlighters rose. For widows, divorcees, and single women, it increased particularly. A series of retail corporations ranging from Avon to Beeline Fashions employ over 50 percent of their staff on a part-time basis. Most of them are moonlighters.

Also, some moonlighting has developed out of economic need. In an age of inflation and increasing taxes, of substandard salaries and unpegged retirement checks, more and more people are seeking extra jobs to help them meet expenses.

If the artisans and the handypersons were the first moonlighters, today's part-time workers are more often academically trained civil servants, teachers, police officers, nurses, clerical workers. It is of interest that teachers are often sought by firms in need of part-time manual labor.

Many moonlighting clerical staff are hired to maintain undeclared books of account. They do not report their additional earnings nor do their part-time employers file tax returns on their businesses.

The temptation for retired people in the United States not to

---

* *Women's Share of Moonlighting Nearly Doubles during 1969–1979,* by Edward S. Sekscenski, Office of Current Employment Analysis, Bureau of Labor Statistics, Washington. The study forms part of an official investigation into moonlighting that indicates that one in twenty gainfully employed also have a second job. This ratio is suspected by many of those interested in the subject of being very much lower than the facts would indicate; there are those who believe that, in fact, a full quarter of the New York labor force free lance on the side. One may, however, assume that there was a similar proportion of men and women who were less than candid in reacting to the survey (see also Chapter 11, pp. 113–114).

disclose income from part-time employment with which they supplement their social security is stronger when they remember that if they earn more than $5500 the benefits will be cut by one-half of their additional earnings.

In an effort to regulate moonlighting and bring it into the monitored economy, Arthur Seldon and others have come up with the proposal that income from overtime should be tax-free. This may sound attractive. It is, however, doubtful whether the idea will ever be put into practice. Politicians will resist it. More seriously, distrust of the establishment today is such that it will take a much more extensive gesture before the members of the subterranean economy decide to surface.

AND WHAT ABOUT BARTER?

The reemergence of barter as an "in" thing is, in a way, unusual. Bartering, often cumbersome, is a very individual method of exchange. One would have thought it runs counter to the age of magnetic tape and computerized business, with the huge amount of matter competing for the time available and filling it up completely.

Like other modes of escape from the clutches of Big Brother, the two sides engaged in barter are expressing their lack of confidence in the system. It is often difficult to define whether barter is an act of evasion or avoidance. Some of it is one of the two, some lies somewhere in between, very close to the dividing line.*

What transactions are, in fact, naturals for barter? Real estate, for one. People swap real estate and oil companies swap oil. Small, medium, and large retailers and wholesalers swap continuously. For years, people have been swapping houses for limited periods. "Paris family looking for an apartment in New York, for the season or the year, offers its own scenic duplex overlooking the Seine in exchange" is a typical example of the classified ads one can read in any one of the daily papers.

---

* William Flanagan describes how limitless the activities of barter are once both sides agree to it in principle. See his "Reintroducing the Barter Economy," in *Subterranean or Underground Economy, Hearings before a Subcommittee of the Committee on Government Operations,* U.S. Government Printing Office, Washington, D.C., 1979, pp. 173–177.

It is estimated that since the end of the 1970s and the start of the 1980s, the barter trade on both sides of the Atlantic has become a multibillion-dollar business which is still growing. For many, it is fun to engage in barter. Families all over the United States are living in houses for which they have exchanged their own. In Salt Lake City and Minneapolis, in Milwaukee and Reston, Virginia, nonprofit clearing houses exist for the purpose of loaning skills, services, and goods on credit.[5]

The rejuvenation of South Street in Philadelphia, Pennsylvania, is a rather striking tale of imaginative barter. Oldtimers will tell you that the street was given a new lease on life mainly because the residents started to exchange goods and services without the use of cash. A typical example is the carpenter who will explain that he has worked on many of the stores in exchange for groceries, liquor, and credit.

Common barter deals are the ones negotiated by Moreton Binn's $5 million annual turnover business in New York, operating under the name of Atwood Richards, Inc., with offices at 99 Park Avenue.[6] Binn has learned that no business operates at 100 percent efficiency: there is always the odd load of slightly flawed merchandise, badly planned advertising space, or other white elephants. He buys it up and sells 10 to 20 percent of it for a cash profit. But what does he do with the bulk? He trades: hockey pucks for plastic mix for television time; the airtime is exchanged for a camera, the camera is exchanged for printing services, the printer gets ocean cruises; the shipping company gets food, the food company gets advertising space on the radio and in a magazine; the magazine traded some of its space for sales meeting rooms at a hotel, the hotel gets wallpaper, the wallpaper company also gets magazine advertising space. And all the deals are worked out through Atwood Richards, Inc., and Binn, the Barter Baron. This is a far cry from the neighbors exchanging baby-sitting services for dressmaking or the CPA doing his ex-wife's tax returns in exchange for some tickets to a football game, but the principle is the same.

AVOISION IN AGRICULTURE

The sector of the economy in which the practice of avoision

through the use of cash and barter is probably the most frequent is agriculture.

Throughout history it has always been difficult to raise any form of public funds from the farming community. Any number of tales are told of villages rebelling against taxation, of farmers who preferred to fight and risk death rather than pay taxes. Taxation caused starvation and emigration; and at times, the central government of the country found it wisest to withdraw the threat altogether.

Modern democracies have proved to be more sensible than to enter into a collision course with the farmers. Although those living gainfully from agriculture are, by law, usually liable for the same tax rates as the rest of us, the authorities are, in practice, tolerant of their nonpayment of taxes. Indeed, many believe it would be too expensive to collect the taxes owed by the farming community; it is preferable to keep them fairly honest by offering them legitimate avoidance schemes. Probably the most successful farmers get the best of both worlds.

Farmers have always made more ongoing barter deals than any other members of the community, and they have no intention of recording any income they may get through it. They may exchange produce for fertilizer, equipment for clothing, and food and lodging for labor. They sell produce on their farms, against cash, with no receipts. In general, their bookkeeping is slack and difficult to audit. And, of course, they enjoy such official perks as accelerated depreciation and other allowances that reduce still further their total net taxable income.

Thus, statisticians and macroeconomists today concede that total agricultural production is larger than national computations indicate. In private, treasury and Internal Revenue Service officials agree that many farmers still maintain a sloppy bookkeeping system, which makes proper auditing difficult, although they are among the few who are allowed to report income on a simple cash basis, rather than on the customary accrual basis. As long as the size of treasury and Internal Revenue Service staff does not grow substantially, auditing the books of the farming community will have low priority. There are more opportunities to underreport farm income than most other forms of income: in most businesses, the purchase of fixed assets is capitalized and then written off over their expected lifespan, but cash accounting allows farmers to write off farm equipment and machinery in the year of acquisition. Similarly, they may write off the cost of developing or improving their orchards, olive groves, or vineyards.[7]

Unhampered by the scanty and ineffective attempts of government to interfere, the cash and barter economy is a growing phenomenon, vital and bustling. Many enjoy taking part in it.

Professor Gutman is right in saying that cash transactions are relatively difficult to trace. But he appears to underrate the ingenuity with which modern business is operating underground. Currency transfers are used in a far more devious way than those transactions in which banking facilities are utilized, and there are any number of ways in which they are of help to the subterranean businessperson. The fact that the underground economy operates through both cash and banking makes measuring it even more difficult. In the United States and certain other countries, it could be considerably larger than Professor Gutman's measurements would have us believe.

REFERENCES

1. Arthur Seldon, *Tax Avoision,* Special Reading No. 22 of the Institute for Economic Affairs, London, 1979, p. 10.
2. See also Richard Upton, "Moonlighting, A Dark Shadow on the White Economy?" *Personnel Management,* March 1980, pp. 28–31.
3. "Au not so Clair de La Lune," *The Economist,* May 5, 1979, p. 95.
4. "A Look at the Nation's 5 Million Moonlighters," *U.S. News and World Report,* December 8, 1980, pp. 49–52.
5. For more information, see "It's Just a Simple Exchange," *Honolulu Star Bulletin,* February 12, 1979.
6. William Flanagan, "Reintroducing the Barter Economy," in *Subterranean or Underground Economy, Hearings before a Subcommittee of the Committee on Government Operations,* U.S. Government Printing Office, Washington, D.C., 1979, pp. 173–177.
7. See also "The Income Farmers Hide," *Business Week,* April 7, 1978, pp. 91, 94.

8

UNDERGROUND GLITTER: ORGANIZED CRIME

There are three things to remember if you have gold fillings: never eat hard candy, don't grind your teeth at night and never smile at a mugger.

—ROBERT ORBEN[1]

NOT ALL DEALINGS IN GOLD AND DIAMONDS ARE UNDECLARED

The diamond trade, including cutters, polishers, merchants, and industrialists, is probably the one single business that has always successfully evaded the inconvenience of paying full taxes on income, whether in the United States, Holland, Belgium, or Israel.

Recorded trading and investment in precious objects has long been common. It was always assumed that diamonds, gold, and other forms of precious jewelry were a convenient disguise for the undeclared income of would-be tax evaders. In the early 1970s, Professor Paul Samuelson wrote that gold was of interest only to hoarders, sheiks, and the underworld. Then, suddenly, the price of gold started climbing very rapidly from its previously steady $35 per ounce until, in 1974, speculation brought it to a peak of close to $180 before it dropped by a third, to $120, where it rested for four years. After the fall of the Shah of Iran, there was another boost, relapse, and rise.*

Still, undeterred, the Nobel Laureate reconfirmed his opinions at the end of April 1980, when he declared that, although hoarders and speculators were still interested in the traditional precious metal, it had no monetary future because it had

---

* The average price of gold at the end of 1980 was 1470 percent more than it had been in 1970, and trading in the metal continued to offer anonymity.

become too unsteady. As a cautious academic, however, he advised investors to put some of their assets in gold and to see in it a hedge against decline in value. He advocated gold bullion coins for the middle-class investor or, in certain cases, shares in goldmining companies.[2]

Trading in gold is made easier by the fact that, eager as they are to hoard this precious metal, Middle Eastern governments often make efforts to conceal the size of their acquisitions and the volume of their trade, buying through agents rather than central banks.[3] It is unclear how much each owns separately, but estimates claim that, in the three years leading to 1980, central governments in the Middle East have bought and hoarded gold equal to forty years of mining in South Africa. Purchases are largely unpublished, sometimes not even reported to the International Monetary Fund. Being substantially larger than the trade in gold by the subterranean economy, the latter's activities are easily submerged in the hidden petrocapital riches.

In countries where there are rigid foreign currency controls, another facet of the unrecorded economy becomes increasingly powerful: smuggling. The smuggling of capital across borders in the form of diamonds, other gems, and gold is an old practice. In periods of twentieth-century crisis and catastrophe it became a chance for survival. Refugees bought their way out of Nazi Germany and subsisted afterwards by selling their jewelry. Smuggling is still a way out of the Soviet Union and other Communist countries, Latin America, and India. But it is not the prerogative of refugees.

When protection and exchange controls were stricter, before telecommunications and the Euromarket, jewelry, especially gold and diamonds, was probably the most popular way of transferring funds across borders. The net value of good jewelry, compared to its size and weight, made it a convenient exchange unit, the presence or absence of which was hard to notice.

The role of gold, diamonds, and other precious stones in the subterranean economy begins at an early stage, long before they become jewelry. It is generally accepted that it is up to the individual diamond or gold merchant to decide whether he or she wants to maintain a full and precise record of business transactions. Few of them would credit any government with the workforce, time, or budget needed to conduct thorough studies of their business. Independent outside control of turnovers and inventories is certainly impossible. Experience also indicates that if any country were to try to lay down the law to its jewelers and their traders, they, rather than suffer the costs of inspection and taxes, would simply pack their bags and move on to a more congenial environment.

WHY DIAMONDS CANNOT BE PROPERLY CONTROLLED

The chief accountant in one of the larger diamond-polishing plants of Amsterdam in the mid-1930s, then a thriving nerve center, recalls his company's good standing and reputation for honesty with the Dutch government. When computing the profits of his employers, the tax inspectors relied heavily on his books of account. Once per year, they would audit and review the books and evaluate the operating results of the company. After a cursory look over their purchases of raw materials from the diamond syndicate, they would assess what the income of the other diamond dealers and industrialists should be. This ex-comptroller, a proud professional and a gentleman of the highest moral principles, then reveals that, like those of their colleagues, his employers' books were cooked; perhaps less so, but still cooked. In no way is it possible to exercise full and effective control from without over the recording of diamond inventories, depletion through polishing, or receipts upon sales.

The Dutch treasury may never have realized that this comptroller was manipulating the inventory records, but they did gradually reach the conclusion that the presence of the tax-evading diamond industry was detrimental to the tax morale of the Netherlands (even then one of the higher tax-collecting countries in western Europe). A couple of years before the outbreak of World War II, the diamond dealers and the administration came to a tacit understanding: virtually overnight, the diamond trade packed its bags and moved across the border to Antwerp, in Belgium, where tax rates were lower, inspectors more tolerant, and the climate friendlier. To date, Antwerp remains the biggest diamond polishing and trading center of the world. For over forty years since, no government has seriously attempted to collect taxes from this sector of the economy. The industry, suspicious as it is and wise to the ways of bureaucracy, has not been taken in by this softness. It remains on the alert, ready and able to pick up and move out of any country where the authorities suddenly become a serious threat.

Whether on 47th Street in Manhattan, in Hong Kong, Bombay, Tel Aviv, or Antwerp, diamond merchants continue not to document sales. They settle a deal with a handshake and the words *Mazal bracha* ("luck and blessings" in Hebrew), and they have no intention to change.

GOLD AND DIAMONDS CAN OPERATE AWAY FROM THE PUBLIC EYE

When the diamonds have been mined, cut, sorted, polished, and traded, they are sold to the public. If they are the larger brilliants, rather than industrial stones, they are bought as a jewelry investment, often for cash. Always in the long run and often also in the short term, their net worth rises faster than the pace of inflation, as demand sharpened by the pressure of undeclared funds exceeds production.

Many of the jeweler's customers are wealthy or middle-class suburban couples. They have saved some cash and are eager to invest it in diamonds. If the acquisition is not documented, so much the better. They buy from the merchant, who got his polished stones from an industrialist, usually an old acquaintance. Following the generations-old custom described above, they shook hands on completion of the deal, leaving no record. The industrialist may have employed several dozen, sometimes hundreds, of cutters, sorters, polishers, and other staff, some with decades of expertise. He records only part of their wages: the minimal amount the tax authorities and social security people will expect. The rest he pays in the form of cash or unrecorded bonuses.

Neither the partner in the prestigious Wall Street merchant bank nor the neatly dressed matron from Westchester County expect the middle-age jeweler on West 47th Street to give them a receipt when they buy a carat ring or expensive necklace. They know he expects them to pay in cash and are not in the least surprised when, poker-faced, he stuffs the wad of banknotes into his pocket, rather than ringing it up on his cash register.

Merchants still carry diamonds on their person when they travel, but with the advent of the telebanking system they enjoy very attractive international banking facilities. The telebanking division is proud of the specialist services it offers and, aware of the peculiarities of the diamond trade, extends what are, in effect, open lines of credit to it. Although there has been an increased number of loans which have turned into losses in recent years, the banking competition is stiff and the bad debts are probably not sufficiently large to convince the bankers of the need to tighten their collateral requirements.

ORGANIZED CRIME

Until now, we have dealt mainly with evasion and avoision, in which tax and currency laws are sometimes broken. (When these activities are illegal, should we call them "soft crime"?)

But the realm of the subterranean economy is much larger and includes other types of activity, stemming from what society usually considers serious "hard" crime.* Indeed, in the failure of democracies to control, measure, or monitor the intermingling of and interaction between crime money and that of the rest of the subterranean economy rests one of the most cancerous dangers to society. Because it has made a thorough study of how to escape most regulatory restrictions and the tax net, organized crime has continued to grow and prosper, while much of the legitimate business world has been simply muddling through what has become chronic stagflation and recession since the mid-1970s. Second in size in the United States only to oil, which showed revenues of $365 billion in 1979, organized crime is accepted as "one of the most powerful forces in the United States today."[4]

One of the difficulties of getting the establishment to comprehend the full extent of the subterranean economy in general and of the crime economy in particular stems from the fact that the funds involved tend to change their characteristics. Monies derived from moonlighting or Mafia funds, prostitution and protection, are often "laundered," that

---

* Funds derived from more or less organized crime all form part of the subterranean economy and warrant separate attention. The comments offered in this chapter and, to a lesser extent, in Chapter 11, describing the hidden economy in the United States, are more a reminder than an attempt to give a fair description of the dynamic, virile, and ominous pace of growth of this money. The attention given here to drug traffic is an example, an attempt to show how funds derived from dangerous crime are, at the same time, often connected with the most respectable financial institutions.

is, turned from "black" to "white," from covert to overt, from unrecorded to fully documented.

There are, however, many other factors that help the parties to the subterranean economy launder their money. For example, a lot of the funds coming through from the tax havens are legitimate; the wish to maintain anonymity is often bona fide. Many funds are drawn to these tax havens from totalitarian or other countries with stringent foreign currency controls. Thus, billions of dollars have reached tax havens from Chile and the Argentine, Brazil and Mexico, Italy and Spain, South Africa, Israel, Iran, and many other countries. They intermingle with the subterranean funds being laundered on the instructions of owners residing in the English-speaking world and northwest Europe.

The principle of laundering is simple. The methods range from the primitive to the sophisticated. At its simplest, it entails the secret transfer of the funds abroad—ostensibly owned now by a foreigner with what may be a fictitious name—and their repatriation. Movement in the opposite direction, when, for instance, income derived from a legitimate business owned by the Mafia is directed to the underground economy, is more complex.

Although there are no precise figures, the size of the Mafia in the United States is thought to be vast. Through its international ties, it is surmised that huge amounts of funds are smuggled out of America to phantom or skeletal destinations in places ranging from the Bahamas and other tax havens to Switzerland. Once these monies have been laundered, they may be returned to the United States to be invested in legitimate businesses. Certainly, far from all the investments made through Swiss banks and trusts in the EEC and the United States in the 1970s is of bona fide indigenous Swiss capital ownership.*

Simple avoision funds benefit in two ways from being deposited abroad: national interest provides relative safety by preventing neighboring countries from making a concerted effort to coordinate their supervision of the flow of money

---

* It is not only funds being repatriated illegally that use a Swiss front. Owners of oil money (mainly Arab), keen to be discreet about their identities, avail themselves of the same facilities. See also Louis Turner, *Invisible Empires,* Hamish Hamilton, p. 79.

across their borders; and many ill-gotten gains stashed away for future enjoyment, such as Mafia money, kickbacks to business agents and their multinational bosses, or even to government officials and ministers of solid, generations-old democracies, are deposited meanwhile in some neutral place. It is also not uncommon for officials from any of the three developing continents, Asia, Africa, and Latin America, to cream off percentages of the aid destined for their countries. In order to get their contracts, businesspeople dealing with the developing countries are often asked to make substantial payments to numbered Swiss bank accounts. The American government came out strongly against this practice in the mid-1970s and, in 1977, Congress enacted the Foreign Corrupt Practices Act. At first it was not realized, but at the end of 1979 there was evidence to show that U.S. companies had lost quite a few contracts in the years following. By 1980, informal steps were being planned to soften the effects of the act. One may suspect that, with the tacit agreement of various government departments, American corporations have decided that it pays to take the risk of contravening the act through foreign subsidiaries and other conduits. Today, they are again getting their fair share of Middle East contracts.

THE DRUG BUSINESS

The whole stratification of dope peddling is outside the legitimate economy. Addicts will, naturally, not acknowledge their spending on drugs; the producers through to the pushers prefer to stay underground.

One of the largest, most successful growth industries in the subterranean economy, in the United States especially, is the drug trade. Florida is popular with drug dealers, who favor it as the marketing center and the base in which to launder illegitimate funds in local banks. Treasury officials, worried by the spread of the drug economy and watching it, have also noticed abnormally large currency surpluses in southern California and places in Texas close to the Mexican border, such as San Antonio and El Paso.

Until federal law required banks to report to the Internal Revenue Service any cash deposits in the excess of $10,000, it was common for blue-jean millionaires to bank huge amounts, sometimes more than a million dollars, in small bills. Lately, drug dealers have become less brazen. "Now you see a lot of deposits for $9999," said Senator William Proxmire, when he was Chairman of the Committee on Banking, Housing and Urban Affairs.[5]

It took the Senate some time before it began its investigations, but it was shocked by what it heard when hearings began, early in June 1980. The drug trade is believed, by some narcotics officials, to be south Florida's biggest business, with a volume in 1979 of at least $7 billion! According to *Newsweek* for June 9, 1980, the figures were much higher. The news magazine cited federal authorities who said that about 70 percent of the estimated $40 billion annual marijuana and cocaine business in the United States (i.e., close to $30 billion!) passed through South Florida.

BANKS AND OTHER RESPECTABLE INSTITUTIONS AID THE DRUG TRADE

Banks have, over recent years, been increasing their active role in servicing this cash flow. Today, they are an indispensible part of the drug trade, according to Jerome Sandford, former Assistant U.S. Attorney, as reported in *The New York Times* for June 5, 1980.[6]

He added that bankers involved in transferring huge amounts of small-denomination bills into easily handled and transferable cashier's checks do so with the risk, at most, of being reprimanded.

The business transactions are mostly computerized. There are rarely any couriers to be kidnapped or cross-border shipments of cash to be seized by customs. The stateside smuggler typically delivers a cash payment to the Miami bank account of a money exchanger who directs the money traffic by wire or telephone for a hefty fee (15 to 25 percent). The go-between then makes the equivalent payment in pesos to the Colombian supplier. If the latter wants to keep his or her money out of Colombia, the exchanger can discreetly have it transferred to an offshore bank account. The agent will also be available to help the American smuggler launder his or her profit and transfer the money to an offshore account.[7]

Whatever its exact size, it is generally agreed that the drug business is flourishing in Miami and that it involves many people, some knowingly, others perhaps not. There are the lawyers, accountants, and other professionals who provide services to the smugglers. Real estate agents and businesspeople sell yachts, planes, expensive cars, and property without questioning the identity of the buyers, who pay them thousands of dollars, cash. Moonlighting airport mechanics are paid handsomely to service planes that can then be used to carry drugs from Colombia; sometimes they are asked to install long-range fuel tanks. And at least six members of the Dade County Sheriff's Office are under investigation for allegedly providing protection to Miami drug dealers . . .[6]

It is almost impossible for federal agents to find out who owns an account or to trace money. Limited manpower and expertise make it a losing battle; they are hopelessly outmaneuvered by some 200 scheming smuggling rings, operating from Miami.* Unless the government steps up its attack, the well-entrenched drug trade is certain to keep on flourishing.

While the successes of the U.S. administration in enforcement are far from glowing, it continues to publish statistics which, until one learns to read between the lines, sound meticulously precise. At the end of August 1979, for instance, the Internal Revenue Service released a report showing that illegal drug sales accounted for $16.2 billion to $23.6 billion in unreported incomes in 1976.

REFERENCES

1. *The Wall Street Journal,* Editorial Page, March 17, 1980.
2. See also H. J. Maidenberg, "Roller Coaster Bullion Prices Left Mining Stocks Unscathed," *The International Herald Tribune,* May 5, 1980, p. 10.
3. "Banks Hoarding Gold Against Inflation," *The International Herald Tribune,* December 27–28, 1980.
4. James Cook, "The Invisible Enterprise," *Forbes,* September 29, 1980, pp. 60–71.
5. "Money 'Laundries,'" *The Wall Street Journal,* September 9, 1980, p. 35.

---

* Toward the end of 1980, there were some signs that the policing efforts in south Florida were having some effect. At least, so it appeared, as drug smuggling was spreading to other parts of the northern Gulf of Mexico.

6. A. O. Sulzberger, Jr., "Banks Help Drug Trade in Miami, Senators Told," *The New York Times,* June 5, 1980.

7. "Miami's Narcobucks," *Newsweek,* June 9, 1980, p. 44.

9

MULTINATIONALS, EUROMARKETS, AND INTERNATIONAL FINANCIAL INSTITUTIONS

THE GROWTH OF INTERNATIONAL TRADE

The arrival of the multinational conglomerate and the tightening of overseas communications among the offices of the big banking houses have created new possibilities of developing sources of undeclared income. In these settings, chief executive officers of multinationals may not always record their approval on paper of the clever, if devious, deals to which they and their top aides are often party. These include the common practice of giving incentives to senior officers of subsidiaries operating in high tax territories and channeling their remuneration into some remote, unreported tax haven. Commission may be granted to preferred clients, even when the American parent corporation is fully aware of the legislation prohibiting such payments. There are other, not quite illegal manipulations and relatively simple forms of avoidance through intercompany billings that reduce the amount of chargeable income in high tax-bracket areas and transmit it to far lower tax-charging countries.

The pace of growth of this new world of business has become far more rapid with the development, in the past generation, of the extraterritorial money market, in which trade worth billions of dollars is carried out without much concern as to what the domicile of the venture is. It is called the Euromarket. Few know that this name does not necessarily refer to a tangible location.

With hardly any government interference, Euromarket trading is carried on in all the financial centers of Europe and as far afield as Tokyo, Los Angeles, New York, and Toronto; as well, of course, as in tax haven centers such as Grand Cayman and the Dutch Antilles.

WHAT IS THE EUROMARKET?

The Euromarket is an international money and capital market that trades currencies outside their countries of origin.[1] It has no geographical definition or demarcation; it is truly international. Eurodollars, for example, the first currency to be used popularly on the Euromarket, are dollar amounts acquired by banks, some of them American, outside the borders of the United States. They are used, either in their original denomination or after exchange into a different currency, in various types of financial operations to grant loans to business and private individuals. Today, the yen and all major western currencies are present in Euromoney and Eurocapital markets, and Arab petromoney has begun to participate, as well. Although ultimately all movement on the Euromarket leads to transfers of assets and liabilities in the countries where the respective currencies originated, there is no system to monitor its daily activities. For, while part of the business carried out in this market is recorded for the computation of national accounts and tax payments, other parts of unknown range remain uncharted.

The multinationals contributed much to the establishment of the Euromarket in the 1950s. In that and the following decade, American business was making large investments in Europe. The American government, however, was enacting measures that made the use of U.S. funds for investment abroad extremely expensive. With the introduction in 1963 of the interest equalization tax (IET), the flow of capital out of the United States almost came to a complete halt. Luckily for the growth of this business, it was discovered that new lines of credit could be raised by Americans more easily through the Euromarket than in their own country.

THE EUROMARKET OFFERED FINANCIAL FREEDOM

The Euromarket offered new financial freedom, including, for instance, the possibility of borrowing in low interest areas and transferring money for operations to higher interest zones. One way of carrying out such transfer pricing[2] could be when a company sells a commodity to a sister company domiciled in a country having a low corporate tax; the sister may then resell to the parent company for the maximum price just below that at which import duty is levied; the go-between, or sister company, thus makes the maximum profit on which the minimum corporate tax rates are payable. These methods were already practiced in the 1960s and put into print in 1968,[3] when a vice president of an American corporation described how the system worked; how, instead of borrowing in its own country at 15 percent, a Finnish subsidiary received money via Sweden and at the third stage from a sister company in Denmark, where the borrowing rate was only 5 to 6 percent. Apart from the saving in financing costs, the maneuver gave the American parent company the benefit of Swedish currency, which, at the time, was stronger than Danish kroner. Such manipulations are quite simple and, more often than not, legal, but still frowned upon by the authorities. They are hard to detect by anyone intent on adding "notional"* income or disallowing expenses in computing the taxable income of one subsidiary or another. When, by means of the above and through transfer pricing, multinationals direct their profits to low tax areas or to other points on the globe where the tax authorities are notoriously incompetent, they contribute to the growth of avoision.

THE BANKS FOLLOW THE MULTINATIONALS

Few sectors of the economy have grown so rapidly or spread as wide in the past generation as the big commercial banks.

Some time after multinational business became common, the bigger American banks started to open branches outside the

---

* The dictionary[4] defines the technical term "notional" as: "Imaginary or unreal: said, for example, of the value of a service not yet rendered, or a liability not yet incurred, but in either case merely in prospect, and hence not to be recorded in the accounts. A long-term lease has been cited as an example of a notional liability."

United States.*

Their foreign activities have grown since 1960 by over 150-fold, from $3.5 billion to more than $500 billion at the end of 1980, and, with them, the contribution of their foreign activities to their profits. In 1970, income from branches abroad represented about 15 percent of the total earnings of the major American banks; by the middle of the decade, they were approximately equal to and often higher than their domestic earnings. In fact, owing to inflation, the real, as opposed to nominal, domestic income of some of the large American banks actually dropped, while their foreign income grew at a rapid pace.

Since the mid-1970s, over half, often as much as two-thirds, of the net earnings of some of the largest banks, such as Citicorp, Bankers Trust, Chase Manhattan, and Morgan Guaranty, are derived from their activities outside the United States.**

They may not always readily acknowledge it, but neither the Federal Reserve Board nor the Bank of England nor the national bank of any other country has any precise knowledge of how many Eurodollars or how much Eurosterling there is, who holds it, or how the funds might enter and influence the American or British economies. It is often difficult to get a clear answer to the question of what the interest-charging policy, monitoring system, or other method of control is of an international corporation or bank with its own offshore bank subsidiary or of one located overseas.

On the face of it, many of these Eurocurrency transactions are very simple: when dollars placed in the Belgian branch of a U.K. bank are loaned to a Brazilian enterprise, they remain Eurodollars. Eurocurrency remains as such as long as it stays

---

* From a virtually insignificant number in 1950, the number of American bank branches, subsidiaries, or affiliates outside the United States grew to 2157 in 1980, compared to the British with 1101 (see *The Economist* Business Brief, December 20, 1980, p. 81). Citicorp is proprietor of about one-half of all the branches of American banks overseas.

** Citicorp, for instance, attributed 71.8 percent and 64.7 percent (close to $900 million) of its net earnings to foreign activities in 1978 and 1979, respectively, and about one-fifth of its earnings are attributable to its business with multinationals. Corresponding figures for Chase Manhattan are 53.2 percent and 46.9 percent; for Morgan Guaranty, 51 percent and 52 percent; and for Bankers Trust Co., 67.9 percent and 51.5 percent. Figures are according to Salomon Brothers and are quoted in the *National Journal* of September 27, 1980.

out of its country of origin and the bureaucrats do not activate their controls. The overhead of gross international foreign banking income is often relatively low, and many banking executives prefer this more "glamorous" line of business to the drudgery of the daily affairs of local branch commercial banking, which deals with many thousands of small depositors.

In itself, the Eurocurrency market is not a part of the subterranean economy, but it does facilitate the conduct of an important segment of the covert business being carried out in the West. Like the unknown quantities of the hidden economy, nobody has any idea how much money there actually is in the Euromarket. As one high bank official put it, the closest one can get is an estimate based on an assumption.[5]

WHERE IS OFFSHORE?

Offshore bases generally mean such localities as the Isle of Jersey, the Bahamas and Cayman Islands, or possibly Hong Kong or Luxembourg. But for many, London provides similar offshore facilities, only more numerous, accessible, and efficient.

Apart from the British banks and their scores of branches, there are over 400 foreign banks operating in London, all offering foreign funding and borrowing services, generally on Euromarket terms. Accounting for one-third of the market, London remains the largest financial center of the world. Indeed, it is so popular that the foreign bankers and their clients are considered to be part cause of traffic congestion at Heathrow International Airport.

While Eurocurrency may include the Euroyen, Euromark, and Eurofranc, the Euromarket language remains English. London supplies the bulk of the clerical, accounting, and legal staff. With sterling weak and dropping, London in the 1960s was a bargain center for the hundreds of banking offshoots converging upon it. In recent years, with sterling overpriced, London is not as attractive as it was, but most bankers believe that the British currency will drop to a more moderate, reasonable level in the not-too-distant future.

Even under a Labor government, British banking regulators and tax authorities remained sympathetic to the foreign financial institutions operating in and from the City. Compared to officials in other European capitals, they are more flexible, less inquisitive, and easier to accommodate.[6]

Encouraged by the advent of the electronic age and as the barrier of fear broke down, a rapid growth became apparent in the activities of the international subterranean economy. With the aid of the extranational market, it is now often possible to get a loan in a New York branch of a French or British bank—and to get it instantly. The money then appears on the books of the European head office as a deposit. A similar transaction may be made by the head office after a deposit liability is converted to an asset in the form of a loan; and the cycle is repeated. These international dealings do not, in the ordinary course of business, come under the close scrutiny of the regulatory authorities, nor are they under the constraint of any liquidity reserve rations* and, more often than not, there is no physical movement of cash. Electronic impulses record the transactions, but some practitioners of avoision no longer have to worry about moving cash-stacked valises across policed borders. The large international banks, with the aid of the Euromarket currency, serve them in almost total security.

Contributing to the growth of nontaxed extraterritorial business are the scores of foreign businesspeople enjoying the still very liberal government approach to the goings-on in the City of London, the somewhat better-controlled financial center of New York, or any one of a number of other business locations, both metropolitan and provincial. Foreigners must have work permits when they operate from Geneva or Zurich, but are rarely required to pay the heavy Swiss taxes. Although citizens living abroad are required by some countries, such as the United States, to file tax returns, they rarely do so in the financial center in which they operate.

No precise information is published as to the individual ownership or origin and use of Euromoney and the Eurocredit markets. The closest to a definitive presentation is made by

---

* Under Regulation D in the United States and a similar one in the United Kingdom, banks are required to maintain a substantial amount of their deposits in nonproductive cash assets. These regulations do not apply to their branches abroad, as the banks argue that they would impair their competitive position. Although governments periodically attempt to intervene and impose a reserve requirement, such attempts have, in fact, been feeble, hesitant, ultimately ineffective, and canceled. Thus, when helped by sound management, foreign activities tend to be more profitable than local operations.

The Bank of International Settlement in Basel. According to the estimates of its economists, the funds are derived principally from

- The Group of Ten and Switzerland
- The oil-exporting countries
- The international organizations

The combined net surplus of claims over liabilities for these three groups amounted to more than $100 billion at the end of 1977 and doubled by the end of 1979. On the borrower's side, there are also certain peak groups, including the developing countries and, mainly, Latin America, eastern Europe, western European countries outside the Group of Ten, and offshore banking centers established in countries with liberal business and tax legislation, including the Bahamas, Barbados, Bermuda, the Cayman Islands, Hong Kong, Lebanon, Liberia, the Dutch Antilles, the New Hebrides, Singapore, and the West Indies.

There is no description of the people behind these statistics. No recognition, for instance, is given to the fact that behind the increased amount of Swiss claims are, at times, funds smuggled out of Latin America or deposited privately by wealthy Arab sheiks.

To date, no regulatory authority, either in the United States or in any of the European Common Market countries, has seriously attempted, in the way they do at home, to monitor or regulate the international activities of any of the equally large European banking institutions, ranging from, for example, Lloyds and the Midland Bank to the Dresdner Bank and the Banque Nationale de Paris. So, in essence, jurisdiction over the larger part of the Eurocurrency remains almost completely in the hands of the banks themselves.

Although, since the collapse of I.D. Herstatt in the spring of 1974,* the banking commissioners of the ten larger western countries (and some of the smaller ones) have been meeting periodically to compare notes on controls, the gaps between the

* This caused losses of DM 1.2 billion owing to currency speculation and fraud and coming as it did in close proximity to the discovery that the Hessische Landesbank had lost another DM 2.2 billion through bad investment and property lending.

different approaches they have on regulation are believed to be quite substantial. It is known that the banking commissioners in the United States believe they have a serious regulatory responsibility and so carry out their regular in-depth reviews of American banks, inspecting their systems and debtor standards. But the British appear to be far more lenient. One of the past governors of the Bank of England, explaining his lack of enthusiasm for the maintenance of a highly qualified and salaried bank audit team, is reputed to have said that a reasonable, independent audit—always a costly thing—will hardly ever prevent a sophisticated fraud scheme and that there is little cause to audit the honest banker. Not surprisingly, it is far easier to parley with their review staff than with their American counterparts—and this consideration is certainly an attraction to foreign banks when they consider establishing a foothold in Britain.

Most international banks today will not object to or seriously query any instructions they might receive from a client which obviously or with hardly any digging indicate that they are intended to circumvent tax or currency exchange laws. No publicity was given to tighter controls introduced in 1978 after a fairly senior official at Citicorp claimed that the Paris outlet of the bank was knowingly, on the instructions of clients, transferring marked-up expense documents to a tax haven affiliate in the Bahamas, thus enabling the clients to smuggle untaxed profits out of France. It is quite clear that the banking regulatory authorities of neither America nor any other nation, nor the independent outside auditors of the international banks themselves, have the capabilities to examine the extent to which the banks promote the free flow of illicity and other funds. Nor do they regard it as a priority to do so.

DOES THE MULTINATIONAL EVADE PAYING TAXES?

One is not always aware of the galaxies of tax consultants retained by the multinational corporations, whose sole job it is to advise them how to reduce their tax liability to a minimum: how legally to avoid as much tax as possible, how to defer the rest for as long as possible, and how to take full advantage of the various tax-law loopholes to help them in their prosperity. These huge corporations generally seem not to actually break the law. If all these devices are used with proper documentation and within the limits of legal and accounting restrictions, the multinational corporation is regarded as shrewd and sophisticated; it presents the image of being somewhat cleverer, with more funds and expense accounts available—all deductible—than its national counterpart which is content to operate in one country only.

Still, evasive practices, some not completely illegal, are often carried out by these businesses. It is, for instance, common practice for officers of multinational corporations, seconded to subsidiaries, to receive part of their salaries in some tax haven, in spite of the fact that the salary is paid by the subsidiary in some form of "overhead" charge to the parent or to an affiliate. An instance of the above manipulations is:

> Through its Dutch subsidiary, a U.S. company named, say, "OCRA,"* which manufactures engines, sells to an African country. To handle the equipment and supervise its maintenance, an African company is established which hires, from its parent and elsewhere, American (and Dutch) executive and engineering staff. The size of the salaries reportedly paid to these foreigners is approximately equal to the direct expenses they incur in this country. There is, however, the additional sum they receive from the group, usually credited to bank accounts they have opened in some safe, tax-free European country. The Dutch company will make this cash transfer out of the overhead fees it has charged the Africans. It is doubtful whether the American parent will publicly show or, indeed, have any written detailed knowledge of which employee was credited with what sum in which country.

The expense incurred by the company or the income of the executives is not technically illegal, and local authorities are probably aware of the arrangements. Such happenings are common. They occur both in developing and in fully industrialized countries and are but one example of a multinational evasive gambit. There are others.

TAX MANIPULATIONS WILL CONTINUE

In theory, one could make a case that, if the tax authorities of a large number of countries get together and agree to a uniform multinational or international tax code with uniform applications of tax principles, such a treaty could reduce

* This name is another figment of my imagination, but the maneuver is frequent with many corporations in situations similar to those described.

manipulations of individual tax systems across national borders. From the jealousy with which the European Common Market members protect their national integrity, one may gather that reaching general international understanding is still a long way off.

In this unpromising, lackadaisical situation, there is little reason for multinationals not to continue to manipulate the price of their products or services. In doing this they are backed by tax lawyers who continuously work on perfecting the use of tax havens. The smallest states and principalities are sometimes the homes of the biggest international giants. Having their name plate in the right places is worth millions of dollars saved in corporate income taxes.[7]

In the 1970s more than before, these corporations availed themselves of the services (mainly in-house) of bright young lawyers and accountants with enough international expertise to advise them on the most advantageous legal way of establishing transfer prices to achieve maximum profit. Naturally, when giving such advice, the consultants take into account not only the tax options, but how to benefit, in this period of escalating inflation and then tumult in exchange rate levels, from the very attractive currency earnings.

The major investors in countries and territories offering tax investment schemes have always been and still are the multinational corporations. According to their strategic planning, the pattern was to set up business in sometimes unusual, but more often than not pivotal, locations and, they hoped, to start accumulating profits as soon as possible. In most cases, the governments of the countries in which the head office, management, and shareholders of the multinational were located paid little attention to the rise in profits of the group abroad. The corporations, on the other hand, rather than repatriate the funds, almost invariably found it preferable to invest them abroad.

Even if, in most cases, they finally have to transfer their earned income to the high-taxing domicile of the parent, the subsidiaries can mostly find reasons for procrastination and use the money for a relatively long time.*

---

* While the cost of international management and controls is frequently greater, it is often easier to make profits in some foreign country where tax rates are

ADMINISTRATIONS APPLY DIFFERENT METHODS IN THEIR ATTEMPTS TO PREVENT INTERNATIONAL AVOIDANCE SCHEMES

In today's world of computerized communications, different countries still define income in different ways. There is rarely agreement as to what constitutes net taxable income or legitimate expenses. Also, with the differing administrative capabilities of the various countries, the actual exchange of data, once agreed upon in principle, may get bogged down in practice. A basic reason for the failure to cooperate is that tax authorities do not agree on exactly what kinds of tax manipulations are unacceptable. Finally, there are often semantic and other technical difficulties that cause breakdowns of communication.

A prerequisite toward establishing international cooperation to reduce both evasion and avoidance is an agreement to exchange information between the tax authorities of various countries. But, in fact, there is hardly any such ongoing collaboration anywhere. Governments do not usually apply the bilateral arrangements offered under the various existing agreements such as those to avoid double taxation.

Tax officials hint that the extent of collaboration based on bilateral treaties is modest. An effective information exchange system would require larger tax audit budgets and the training of staff—at present nonexistent. The treaties were originally signed to guarantee that income be taxed only once, but, with the prohibitive level of taxes and the ingenuity of well-paid tax consultants, in many cases income is not taxed at all.

Still, the tax authorities keep trying. Some countries (e.g., Germany and, in a less effective way, France), when they can get the information, disregard the sham tax haven corporations or trusts and attribute the income to taxable nationals. The United States is powerful enough to make the tax haven (e.g., the Netherland Antilles and Grand Cayman) charge higher tax on earnings derived from American residents.

The very approach toward avoidance and tax reduction schemes differs greatly from country to country. In Britain, the

---

lower or the authorities are less zealous in applying the tax laws, than at home. In other cases and countries, business conditions are simpler than at home, increasing the chances of making a profit. (See footnote to p. 80, "Under Regulation D. . . .")

letter of the law usually prevails. In France, a taxpayer may be accused of "abusing his or her rights"; in Holland, of committing "legal fraud"; in Australia and New Zealand he or she may fall foul of "annihilation clauses"—all without technically breaking the law. The OECD is trying to work out some standard request forms for the exchange of tax data, but the more advanced tax authorities will continue to be impatient with the inability of others, such as Italy, to provide quid pro quo. The OECD is also trying to define the elusive face of tax avoidance, but it will be a long time before agreement is reached.

On the exchange of data, *The Economist* wrote that the United States, the United Kingdom, and West Germany "have expanded informal working arrangements under bilateral tax treaties to permit some simultaneous audits. Canadian and American officials have been doing this for years."[8] But no data have been published indicating the effectiveness of this cooperation and, in private, senior Internal Revenue staff concede that the contemplated mechanism is, in fact, still far from being realized.

It is often asked why more serious attempts at cooperation are not made. There are a number of explanations. For instance, the one that, "in an increasingly internationally minded world, taxing remains a bastion of national sovereignty and breaches of taxpayers' privacy are not lightly explained to voters." Also, many countries, including Switzerland, remain eager to make money from foreign tax dodgers. While willing to sign a plain document that will condemn the principle of evasion, such countries often refuse to join the more rigorous tax conventions that would provide active bilateral control of evasion.

There are exceptions. The government of the United States tried some arm-twisting on the Swiss to learn of Mafia and other funds deposited in their country in the 1970s. The Swiss, uninterested in the source of the monies deposited in their bank accounts, objected in principle to the American intrusion. In specific cases, however, without jeopardizing the general rule, they did provide some information to the inspectors from New York.*

---

* This was largely due to the persistence in the early 1970s of Robert M. Morgenthau and Whitney North Seymour Jr., then attorneys of the Southern District of New York.

THE U.S. TREASURY (SOMETIMES) ENCOURAGES THE SUBTERRANEAN ECONOMIES OF OTHER NATIONS

Well known are the strong objections of the American administration to the Swiss secrecy laws which hinder it in carrying out any effective investigation of the funds the American citizen is suspected of hiding.

What is less well known is that the treasury of the United States quietly helps the American economy to absorb many dozens and possibly well over a hundred billion dollars, mostly smuggled out from the Latin American countries but also including, most probably, unrecorded monies earned within the United States. By permitting offshore banking activities in, for instance, Grand Cayman, Bermuda, and the Bahamas, operated from New York, Miami, and Montreal, the American government offers at least tens of thousands of depositors a technical device which helps them preserve their income without officially having to record it.

The Argentine economy is going through a novel experience. Many small- and medium-size industries are going out of business, while the army and the civil service are growing in size. Unemployment is still increasing rapidly and many local banks are going bankrupt. But the foreign banks are thriving, showing what their headquarters regard as splendid returns. Although, in theory, every citizen may officially take out of the country a sum equal to $20,000, most prefer to continue what they regard as the safer method of smuggling cash out, rather than putting their export of funds on record. The reason being that the right to export capital is not fully spelled out in the law but in a Junta ordinance, which may be changed overnight. There are no details as to how often one may export such an amount: Every day? Once per year? Once in a lifetime? And in general the feeling is that the Junta, like all such authoritarian bodies, is unpredictable: the less contact one has with it, the better.

Very few of the international banks have any of their staff actually smuggling funds abroad or carrying out any other acts which are locally regarded as illegal. A way in which clients get their money out of a Latin American country and into foreign hard currency deposits is as follows:

A client shows up and describes his wish. The bank suggest that he contact an intermediary, possibly a travel or shipping agent, usually a native of the same South American country.

This agent has a deposit account in Zurich, Miami, or New York, probably with an offshore office of the main bank. He buys from the client the local currency and instructs the bank abroad to pay him the equivalent out of his deposit with them. It is, almost always, a very smooth operation.

Unlike the tough governments of the Argentine, whose Junta is not fully trusted by the population, Brazil, or Chile, the government of Uruguay is supportive of the completely free currency and banking the multinational Euromarket community has developed there over the years. With the virtual disappearance of the Tupamaros, the urban guerrillas, and an acceptable degree of runaway inflation, Montevideo, some 120 kilometers across the La Plata River from the Argentine, is booming.

Argentinians, Brazilians, or Chileans do not always jump as far as to the offshore islands of the United States. Many feel comfortable and almost as safe using Uruguay as their tax haven and depositing their funds in international bank branches there.

Some of the largest banks in the world, such as Barclays Bank in Great Britain, Citicorp in the United States, and the West German Dresdner Bank, actively, if not quite openly, guide Argentinians and other South Americans in their quest to transfer some of their savings out of their own countries. They are enjoying very substantial profits from their operations in South America.

OTHERS PREFER TO TRANSFER PART OF THEIR CAPITAL FURTHER NORTH OR NORTHEAST

There were, in the summer of 1980, 357 *(three hundred and fifty-seven!)* banks operating on the Cayman Islands,* the total population of which is all of 20,000, living mainly in

---

* That is, there is a bank office for every 56 Cayman Islanders, compared to 1 per 13,000 Swiss, 4000 Britishers, or 6025 Americans. To put it differently, there are 109 foreign bank subsidiaries, affiliates, or branches operating in Switzerland, 409 in the United States, and 636 in the United Kingdom. (See *The Economist* Business Brief, December 20, 1980.)

Georgetown. The banking presence in the nearby, somewhat larger, Bahamas is just as lively. The banks are connected electronically to their mainland affiliates. They keep up-to-date books of account and pay proper taxes on their own net earnings derived in the United States.

These offshore banks are not subject to any liquidity requirements, and all funds deposited may be put to productive use in the form of loans and similar lines of credit; earnings by the depositors derived from deposits are not taxable.*

Nor do the depositors or their financial activities risk being exposed to the authorities in either the United States or any Latin American country.

The mainland offices or affiliates of the offshore banks, in New York or elsewhere, have a full and detailed record of the offshore member of their family and its banking activities. Depositors need not, and hardly ever do, stop over on the island, but they frequently visit the bank in the United States to be updated on the state of their investments, to sign the appropriate documents, and to give instructions concerning their discretionary accounts. Many of their investments are made through the acquisition of Certificates of Deposit, considered a liquid and safe negotiable instrument.**

An unknown proportion of the deposits with these offshore banks is made by citizens of the United States. Some of them are fully recorded and made with the sole purpose of enjoying the higher yields available through these banks, but others are derived from unrecorded sources within the United States.

Tax absolutionists might call these arrangements sham, but there is no evidence to date that, as a substantial part of these funds are invested in the United States, the administration is overfussed and bothered by them, so their further growth may be expected.

---

* This is one of the inducements to transfer subterranean (untaxed) earnings to offshore havens. Future profits derived from such investments will not be taxed at all or, at the most, will be charged at a minimal rate.

** A Certificate of Deposit, or "CD," is a receipt for a deposit of dollars or some other hard currency made with the bank. The document states the interest rate at which the deposit was made and on which date the bank will repay the money. It is freely marketable.

REFERENCES

1. *The Euromarket,* UBS Publications on Business, Banking, and Monetary Problems, Vol. 62, 1978 gives this and other details.
2. See Louis Turner, *Invisible Empires, Multinational Companies and the Modern World,* Hamish Hamilton, London, 1970, pp. 76–78.
3. *Fortune,* September 15, 1968, pp. 75–76.
4. Kohler's *Dictionary for Accountants,* 3d ed., Prentice-Hall, Englewood Cliffs, N.J., 1963.
5. J. L. Davis, "Banker's Casino—Gambling in the $900 Billion Euromarket," *Harper's,* 1980, pp. 43–57.
6. *The Economist,* November 29, 1980, p. 24.
7. See also Richard J. Barnet and Ronald E. Muller, *Global Reach,* Simon and Schuster, New York, 1974, p. 36.
8. *The Economist,* March 22, 1980, p. 69.

10

TAX SHELTERS, HAVENS, AND HOLIDAYS

The popular press has been devoting more and more space to describing just how both the jet set and the political leadership enjoy the advantages of tax shelters. *Time* magazine devoted a full page to how Ronald Reagan and Jimmy Carter benefited from Internal Revenue Service rules to help them save thousands of tax dollars on their personal holdings. Teddy Kennedy uses real estate as his tax shelter. The magazine goes on to quote the publisher of a tax shelter newssheet in Valley Forge, Pennsylvania, as explaining that more and more people are turning to tax shelters because inflation has blown up their incomes until they reach the 50 percent bracket; about 2 million American tax returns now come into this category.[1]

Benefiting from tax shelters is not the monopoly of Americans or their leaders. It is probably done more frequently and far more extensively by the wealthy French, for whom it is not *comme il faut* to pay taxes in any substantial amounts. In the past decade, for instance, much publicity was given to the tax avoidance schemes of former President Valéry Giscard d'Estaing (see also Chapter 12) and of two former Prime Ministers: Jacques Chaban-Delmas and Jacques Chirac. There is no evidence that either their careers or their private lives were, in any way, affected by this publicity, even though some papers gave critical reports of the proceedings.

Most British leaders are believed to be more discreet. There have been only a few stories of politicians taking advantage of tax shelters. More publicity has been given to the cleverly structured estate duty avoidance schemes of some peers and to personalities in the arts who became expatriates in order to enjoy the economic advantages of life in some tax haven (see p. 104).

It is common among social welfare economists of the West in general and the United States in particular to oppose the possibilities of resorting to tax avoidance schemes. The subject received a somewhat personal exposure with the case of Donald Regan, chief executive officer of Merrill Lynch until selected by President Ronald Reagan to be his first secretary of the treasury. In his earlier position, Donald Regan actively pushed tax avoidance schemes, such as those using commodity straddles, which enabled investors to take a tax loss one year and delay the tax profit to the next. The program may have "cost" the American administration $4 billion in 1980, and the Internal Revenue Service has been seeking ways to brand it as illegal.[2] The moral and social conflict between supervising the federal tax system and encouraging, until recently, the legitimate avoidance schemes could present Donald Regan with questions difficult to answer.

TAX AVOIDANCE SCHEMES

The discovery of avoidance schemes involving tax havens has, over the years, irritated the fiscal authorities; if it smelled a juicy story, the popular press was always happy to give full exposure to the conflict. In the United Kingdom, probably the record ongoing confrontation between the government and a successful tax-avoiding family has been that with the Vesteys, headed by the late Lord Vestey and Sir Edmund Vestey. In 1921, long before the enactment of antiavoidance legislation became an annual happening in Congress and Parliament, the Vesteys had the foresight to set up a family trust in Grand Cayman. As a result, this very wealthy family has, for over sixty years, legally avoided paying almost all taxes, while the British treasury tries to "do something" about it. Over the years, the efforts of the chancellor of the exchequer have at times been quite grotesque, with talk, in 1980, of introducing retroactive legislation to bag some of their income.

For every tax law there is a loophole. The net result of the many anti-anti-anti-tax-avoidance provisions introduced into the British and, later, the American tax codes has been to make many tax avoidance consultants very wealthy.

There are ways and means of reducing the tax burden, even in those countries with the steepest taxes and the most efficient collection system. Anybody who has had any experience of the subject knows that there is always a way around tax legislation for those who really seek it.[3]

In the international tax departments of the large multinationals and in some of the well-endowed university business schools, imaginative research and development teams can, and do, think up avoidance schemes which are easily light-years ahead of government efforts to close tax-law loopholes. This is not because the bureaucrats in Washington or elsewhere lack zeal or ambition. In theory at any rate they do not. Many tax enforcers are capable, intelligent, solid professionals, well-versed in the complicated verbosities of bureaucratic jargon. They deal ably, if dully, with the conformist, familiar elements of the Tax Code and its application, but they are certainly not trained to anticipate what the brilliant, sometimes adventurous avoidance consultant will advise his or her client. Nor has the tax system got either the budget to combat clever, well-thought-out avoision schemes or the glamor to attract enterprising young people to its ranks. It is rare for a creative mind to want to join the civil service or to have the patience needed to sustain its owner as he or she moves slowly up the rungs of the establishment ladder.

Invariably, there are more international tax avoidance possibilities than there are tax laws and regulations. With the growth and intensification of international business, more imaginative and sophisticated than the laws designed to prevent international tax avoidance, the extent and variety of the avoidance schemes continue to proliferate.

Owing, in part, to the secrecy surrounding the international tax practice of any one individual, knowledge of which is restricted to tax officials and personal advisers, it is unlikely that the shortfalls and arbitrariness, ineffectuality and partiality of the international tax laws will be corrected in the foreseeable future.[4]

THE TAX HAVEN

The term "tax haven" applies to countries in which income tax, if it exists at all, is low or which offer other tax advantages. Tax havens usually also offer financial secrecy backed by laws which hinder officials of high tax or authoritarian countries from investigating the activities of their citizens residing in a more generous second home.

Few doubt that tax havens have become big business in recent decades. There are any number of visitors to these bustling hideaways. From Grand Cayman to Lichtenstein, from Luxembourg to the New Hebrides, there are countries which offer their flags of convenience to anybody wishing to reduce his or her tax burden. The most reputable of the legal firms and, naturally, also the Big Eight accounting firms, as well as the second tier of both professions, all have their international tax consultants whose job it is to figure out how to do it all legally. The larger banks have all, by now, established branches, subsidiaries or affiliates in some tax haven through which they offer tax-free security to the investor who can afford it.

A number of guidebooks have been published on the subject. There is Grundy's *Tax Havens,*[5] which describes the attractions and costs to be expected when investing in Jersey, Liberia, the New Hebrides, or other minute points on the globe. *The Economist* Intelligence Unit Ltd. has published an advertisement offering, for $44 or £20, their booklet on *"Tax Havens and Their Uses."*[6] In their Special Report No. 61 they claim to show what tax shelters have to offer both the individual and the corporation and to survey the tax haven scene, past, present and future.

The simplest way for a merchant, trader, importer, or exporter to transfer funds from a high-tax country or one with stringent foreign currency controls to a tax-free haven with minimal control is by transfer pricing manipulation. This normally involves adjusting prices to keep profits out of the more demanding territory. It is a habit-forming policy, not only in South Africa and Latin America but also for many businesses in the United States, the United Kingdom, and western Europe, from where senior executives are happy to visit Switzerland from time to time to collect the profits deposited in their companies' Swiss bank accounts.

Offshore tax havens, which have, by the way, made many tax consultants quite wealthy, became popular when it was proved that some of the schemes involving them kept income away from the long arm of the taxman. Today, in spite of the efforts of their Inland Revenue Service to the contrary, the British tolerate the system better than the Americans. As we saw in connection with the Vesteys mentioned previously, in appeals by the British revenue authorities to the courts, the law lords stick to the form of the transaction rather than considering the substance. In the United States, the tax authorities have been waging a vocal war against these operations. Recent rulings have given more attention to what the motivation behind the schemes was. If the Internal Revenue Service succeeds in proving that the sole purpose for the transaction was to avoid tax, the offshore nature of the deal could well be ignored and the proceeds fully taxed. Still, this form of avoidance is common and possibly growing in frequency and volume.

"TAX PLANNING" IS A EUPHEMISM

Like the wealthy individual and the successful business, the multinational corporation continues with its long- and short-range so-called tax planning, which is a euphemism for "tax *avoidance* planning."

"Tax planning" and "cash flow strategy" do not only mean ways of charging raw materials and finished goods as profitably as possible to the multinational; they also include manipulations of long- and short-term credit policies, rates of interest on credit received and the pace of repayment to the parent or some affiliated company, and close supervision of the repatriation policy of all uncommitted cash surpluses accumulated in the ordinary course of business.

It is sometimes possible to borrow in low-interest areas and transfer the proceeds to high-interest zones. Such movements of capital are relatively simple to make but hard to detect, even assuming that the government is trying to scrutinize the group's activities. A subsidiary in one country might be instructed to stop borrowing while another, in a low-interest area, will be asked to borrow for both.

A well-integrated multinational can manipulate the costs of transactions between one nation and another. It may, for instance, instruct its subsidiary in a high-tax area to buy more expensively from one subsidiary and sell cheaply to another, in a low-tax area.

These policies are influenced not only by tax considerations but also by inflation, by the fluctuating value of the local currency, and, ultimately, by the danger of devaluation which has, since the late 1960s, been facing what were previously considered hard currency economies.

To the reader with an interest in finance, material published on tax planning is often as titillating as were the naughty magazines of a generation ago, when moral censorship in the United States and the United Kingdom still prohibited the full display of naked bodies and bare bosoms were unheard of.

A quite typical example is the pamphlet describing the Seventh Annual Conference of the International Tax Planning Association, held in Montreux, Switzerland, between May 20 and 22, 1981. It begins by emphasizing that "none of [the] material [presented at the conference] is available in published form. . . . The opening papers [are] on the use of partnerships in international tax planning, that tackle an almost unexplored subject. . . ." It goes on to describe another "speaker . . . who practises in Calgary, Alberta. In recent years, that province has attracted a very great deal of international investment and much attention has been given to structuring oil and gas investment in such a way as to afford the foreign investor the benefit of tax advantages not only in Canada but in his home country." The speaker "will indicate the most favorable structures to be adopted by investors in Germany, the U.K., the U.S. . . . and . . . other capital-exporting countries. . . . The starting point of the second talk . . . is the material which emerged from the extremely stimulating workshop held in Monte Carlo" (where else?) "in September, 1980 . . . [when] the main uses of insurance to taxpayers in various jurisdictions . . . [will be discussed]." And so it continues at some length.

On another page, the writer declares that the purpose of the association, which was founded in 1975, is "the study of international tax planning and matters related thereto." He points out that "membership is normally open to those who satisfy the Committee that their work is, in its normal course, concerned with or includes the theory or practice of International Tax Planning or the study thereof, *but it is not concerned with and does not include, whether or not as the employee of any government, levying taxes of any kind in any part of the world."* (My emphasis.)

TAX HAVENS SHOULD OFFER SAFETY

Confidence in the tax haven is of prime importance. The Swiss banks have, over the years, managed to impress this upon their financial clients. There is little doubt that they are fully aware of the protective cloak their discretion offers and how it manages to hide the very funds regarded by the governments of friendly neighbors as criminal. The following anecdote, described by H. J. Browning,[7] illustrates the concept of Swiss safety. Apparently, when Mr. Browning was deputy chief investigation officer in British Customs and Excise, he visited the offices of his Swiss counterparts and asked for their help in locating an individual who was planning to defraud British Customs by means of false documents issued in Switzerland. Mr. Browning knew who and where the prospective criminal was. All he wanted was help in preventing him from carrying out his scheme.

The Swiss reaction was a polite refusal. They also enquired whether, perchance, on his way to meeting with them, the British customs official had not done anything for which, according to Helvetian law, he could be arrested. Mr. Browning beat a hasty retreat.

It would appear that their reputation for discreet handling of funds deposited within their borders is more important to the Swiss than any questions of morality that others might see fit to raise. After the big Chiasso scandal of 1977 involving the Banque Crédit Suisse, one of the three largest commercial banks in the country, the Swiss banks signed an agreement with their national bank not to accept illicit funds knowingly. It is assumed that they will now, in practice, refrain from doing business with notorious criminals, but will continue to serve others as usual. The understanding has not stopped the flow of unmonitored funds into Switzerland, but there is evidence to show that the bankers are more careful. A report published late in 1980 shows that a certain degree of supervision is in effect, but capital flowing into Helvetia still evades currency controls.[8]

Even if one is not quite as sure as in the past just how discreet Swiss banks are, they do make considerable efforts to reduce the size of the activities of their clients. A large part of the client funds handled by the Swiss banks are not shown in their financial statements; very little public reference is made to them. The funds are usually in the form of trust deposits amounting to anywhere between five and ten times the size of the deposits actually shown in the balance sheets. This money may be invested in various businesses by the banks, either following explicit instructions or through their general discretionary powers, officially at depositors' risk. Such investments often show a higher return than usual, but are also somewhat more risky. The aggregate size of the trust deposits and similar funds form one of the larger single economic elements operating in the Euromarket, through which flow both recorded and, to a greater degree, unrecorded funds from all continents. In recent years, increasing amounts of Arab petrofunds have been passing this way.

Not everyone realizes how easy it is to have a simple tax shelter, and it might be of help at this point to try to define what a tax shelter actually is. Briefly, it is a transaction in which the law (intentionally or otherwise) permits a deliberate mismatching of costs and revenues: expenditures ordinarily considered to be of a capital nature are allowed as tax deductions.

While it is easy to have one, tax shelters do, however, have a tendency to become complicated. What happens, for instance, when a West German patentee, seeking to license a U.S. company, is reluctant to submit to U.S. or West German tax? He might take the following steps:

1. Assign patents to a Lichtenstein holding company incorporated as an "Anstalt."
2. Lichtenstein Anstalt grants license to a Swiss letterbox company, which, in turn, licenses a U.S. corporation.
3. The U.S. corporation pays royalty to the Swiss corporation; royalty is free of U.S. withholding tax by virtue of U.S.–Switzerland tax treaty.
4. The Swiss company pays equivalent royalty to Lichtenstein Anstalt; Switzerland levies no withholding tax and the Swiss holding company pays no Swiss profits tax (because its income and expenses cancel each other out).
5. Lichtenstein Anstalt pays no profit tax (merely net worth tax

of 0.1 percent per annum) and no tax on distribution of profits; it accumulates royalties until its West German owners require them.

6. If the West German company in fact owns the U.S. corporation, they ensure that royalty rate is high and absorbs as much U.S. profit as possible.

Shelters were originally established to encourage various types of investment which were thought to be of public interest, ranging from exploration for natural resources and their development to public housing, construction, and equipment leasing. Often, these investments are risky and would not be made without tax incentives; a considerable amount of time may pass before they generate income, if they ever do. But, thanks to the tax shelter arrangement, the taxpayer may, meanwhile, set them off against other income, derived from completely unrelated sources.

In short, tax shelters are investments that enable people to generate paper losses to write off against their regular income. They shield the investor's profit from the full bite of the income tax authorities. Tax shelter schemes do not stipulate that investment be made in the home country. Most wealthy countries, ranging from the United States to West Germany, encourage investments under various limiting conditions in developing and other countries.

It is typical of modern bureaucracy that, through the tax shelter, many projects have been set up in recent years that do little for the economy or are not within the interests of the legislature. In fact, the variety of tax shelters is only limited by the ingenuity of the tax consultants who think them up.

The aims of the rich industrialist multinationals, some of which are conglomerates, are hardly those of the tax-avoiding individuals relaxing on a subtropical island; here, growth, dynamic activity, sales, revenue, profits, and the like, all in excess of what can be expected in even a sophisticated home country, are of primary importance. These possibilities can be found in the European Common Market countries and other advanced economies, as well as in younger growth economies with a substantial national development budget and an equally impressive tax code, often carrying with it what appears to the industrial multinational to be an attractive investment encouragement scheme.

SO, TAX HAVENS CAN BE FUN, BUT NOT ALWAYS

Many tax havens for individuals are located in subtropical parts of the world.

With the main exception of Switzerland, which has one of the most sophisticated economies, Lichtenstein, the Channel Islands,* and Luxembourg, all close to the capitals of central Europe and the centers of international business, most of the tax havens which have become well known during the past two decades are at least several hours by plane from New York, London, Paris, or Frankfurt, but communications with them are usually fairly easy. The affluent individual expects currency to be freely convertible in the tax haven, the cost of living reasonable, and manual labor available for personal services. In countries where some tax system exists, it will be minimal; a double taxation relief agreement with his or her country of origin is not customary. Such out-of-the-way havens include Bermuda, the Bahamas, the Cayman Islands, Curaçao, Panama, and the Virgin Islands in and around the Caribbean; Hong Kong, Singapore, and the New Hebrides in the Far East; and the Seychelles in the Indian Ocean. It could well be that, when the turbulence subsides, Lebanon, Cyprus, and Malta along the Mediterranean coast will resume their economic role and financial growth.

The minimal tax rates, which are the attraction of tax havens for the rich individual, are usually expected to last at least a generation. Nations aiming to attract foreign business usually offer tax incentives with a shorter lifespan; with major changes expected in their social and economic positions, many countries are expected to alter their incentive policy after ten to fifteen years, and each tax haven no doubt has its own advantages and its own drawbacks.

Heads of corporations first setting out on the search for territories and properties for investment often discover that behind the glamor of a tax haven there lurks a bumbling, ineffective, often unsympathetic bureaucracy and a difficult, unresponsive labor force. Even experienced directors of global companies are sometimes guilty of less-than-satisfactory research into the implications of investing in some new

---

* Until the 1960s, Monaco was also regarded as a haven, and there are still a few other possible "close-by" havens, such as San Marino and the Vatican in Italy, the Isle of Man, and Andorra in the Pyrenees.

territory. In the 1960s, a number were seduced to the charms of sunny Italy by the very stimulating incentive program the Italian government had prepared for the development of the Mezzogiorno, the whole poorer section of Italy, south of Naples to Sicily. A few years later, they found themselves having to cut their losses and leave. In the 1970s, fratricide in Lebanon and the destruction of the business center in Beirut caused the evacuation of the growing number of foreign businesses that had been set up there. By the end of the decade, quite a few European bases of American multinationals in search of lower costs were moved from Switzerland to less expensive European centers.

It should be clear that an investment in some faraway country can only be said to pay off after expending the cost of supervising it. This latter usually rises in almost direct proportion to its geographical distance from the controlling parent.

The corporation is out to get the highest return for itself. Although corporation officers make some efforts to minimize the importance of this fact, when the options are open, most multinationals enter the country which offers maximum incentives and possibilities to promote their business and where they stand to pay insignificant taxes, if any. If the host country receives any benefit, the multinational will bask in the ensuing publicity and will happily make the most of this bonus. It will, as far as legally possible, avoid paying taxes through a series of intercompany transactions and similar gambits which may reduce local profits, but will increase those of the group. When multinationals sense a danger that the business investment climate is changing or that they may become liable for heavier taxes than they are willing to pay, they may well decide to reduce their commitments in that particular country.

Before moving into a new country, the multinational will check the encouragements the prospective host government has to offer: tax shelters, tax holidays, tax deferrals, incentive grants, long-term low-interest loans, and so on.

The ideal country for the multinational to invest in would be one where the currency is undervalued, the trade unions cooperative and progressive, taxes low to moderate, and the growth potential promising.

HOW DOES THE HOST COUNTRY ATTRACT FOREIGN INVESTMENT?

A host country has a set of legal instruments with which to expand or curtail the benefits granted and thus to control or encourage foreign investment. These include the actual tax laws and "tax holidays" offered, as well as the various types of investment grant, which differ substantially from country to country, but all contribute to lowering the cost of the fixed assets, often to below international competitive free market rates. There are further incentive schemes for the preferred enterprises, in the form of rebates of and exemption from excise and customs duties and other indirect taxes.

National or regional tax incentive schemes are generally considered to come under the caption of tax avoidance. They usually relate to the encouragement of investment and have two phases: the investment phase and the operational phase. A typical first-phase package will include offers of government grants and subsidized, low-interest loans; a suitable infrastructure will often be available. Once the plant commences operations, for a medium-term period it will enjoy reduced added tax on products sold, as well as the accelerated depreciation which enables a profitable business to defer its tax liabilities; there will sometimes be lower income tax levies, as well. Incentive programs are also common to help attract and train staff. Typical of such schemes are those of the West Berlin Economic Development Corporation and the Irish Industrial Development Authority. (See the IDA's pamphlet describing terms offered.) But they also exist in many other areas where the normal cost of investment and prevailing tax rates would otherwise discourage potential investment. Government incentive schemes vary considerably. Attractive incentive offers have been made by countries ranging from the United States to Israel and from the developing republics of South America to the emerging African states. They often include elements like the following:

Tax Exemption

Profits derived from the export of goods made in the tax haven may get total relief from the taxes of that country for, say, fifteen consecutive years and partial relief for, say, a further five years.

Manufacturers from abroad may repatriate dividends and

profits in the currency of investment, free of taxes or any other levies. The same applies to capital and appreciations thereon.

Cash Grants

Cash grants may be provided toward the cost of the fixed assets of new industrial undertakings. These grants need not be repaid. They may consist of up to 50 percent in certain preferred investment areas, up to 35 percent in others, on up to a certain prearranged ceiling over which special arrangements may be reached.

International tax specialists usually advise the multinational parent and help it establish what, to the outsider, looks like a rather complicated structure, the main purpose of which is to pay the minimum amount of taxes in the various countries in which the primary profit centers operate. In many countries, rather than avoid all taxes by showing a "carry-forward tax loss" it is common to advise that at least a symbolic tax be paid to the local authorities. Apart from that, the advice is to get all possible profits out of the country as fast as permissible, remembering that corporate strategy invariably attempts to increase the group's total effectiveness on world markets, rather than having tax avoidance as its principal object. In the course of the ensuing tax planning, considerations are weighed concerning, for instance, the existence and advantages of prevailing double tax relief agreements, (common mainly between countries with high taxation rates); or whether investments should be made through tax haven corporations. If the latter, which ones? The rigors of foreign currency controls are evaluated, the gross tax on distributed dividends compared to management fees. . . . After investments are made and production is in full swing, the condition of the subsidiary and its tax position should be reassessed periodically.[9]

The Irish have been fairly successful in their incentive program, bringing a respectable amount of foreign investment from the United States, West Germany, and other countries into theirs.

Among their more attractive projects was one to persuade artists, preferably of Irish descent, to settle in Ireland by providing tax-haven facilities. Quite a few availed themselves of this offer. For some time, John Huston, the film producer and director, was one of them, as was J. P. Donleavy, author of *Beastly Beatitudes of Balthazar B.* and *The Ginger Man.*

Some artists prefer Switzerland: Yehudi Menuhin settled in Gstaad, the late Charlie Chaplin chose to live on the Lake of Geneva. Others, such as the late Noel Coward and Ian Fleming, went for the Caribbean. Arthur Hailey, the meticulous author of *Airport,* among other books, is based in the Bahamas. A few years ago, he delivered an after-dinner speech to an international assembly of auditors and tax consultants at which I was present. It was a lucid, technical description of his trade, commencing with how he sets out to collect material and ending with how he carefully weighs the legal tax advantages of his new "sure" bestseller and why his offshore base close to the United States is the most attractive domicile for him. When he completed his talk, we in the audience knew we had met a first-class husbander of resources.

VENTURE CAPITAL TAX SHELTERS

Venture capital tax shelters have become very popular in recent years. Most attracted to them are self-made millionaires looking for specially tailored tax situations, such as research and development (R & D) tax shelters. One example of such is the project developed by John DeLorean to produce a completely new car to be manufactured in Northern Ireland. Investors were required to put up $150,000 each. In return, they received not shares, but the prospect of future special tax benefits not otherwise available. Compared to the nearly $25 million invested by the private financiers and the research partnership and another $4 million put up by John DeLorean himself, the $147 million of taxpayers' money which the British government injected into the project in its effort to encourage the promoters to establish their plant in Ulster was a significant contribution. The reasons were socioeconomic and political: to increase employment in an economically depressed area. Ultimately, the tax shelter scheme should also prove beneficial to the capital behind Mr. DeLorean.[10]

Another case was the $30 million raised in 1980 to advance the Lear Fan turboprop aircraft. The money of the investors was to be used to carry out all the tax-deductible research and development on the airplane, which would then be sold against royalties. As well as claiming tax deductions on the research and development of the airplane, the investors may also pay capital gains tax, which is much lower than income tax, on their royalties. And the entrepreneur is happy because he does not have to share his company with anybody.

Periodically, the media come out with lurid exposures of tax-haven and tax-shelter manipulations. When loud enough, they are followed by questions in the House or investigations in Congress, and pious administration commitments to deal with the matter "seriously." It is, however, almost certain that pressure from hardship areas will continue and that "bonanzas" will go on being offered.

With recession and economic pessimism as hot political issues, sophisticated tax dodges (at least for individuals) have gone off the boil. Internal Revenue Service officials prefer to concentrate on simpler matters and to hunt easier prey, such as housepainters, greengrocers, and other rank-and-file members of the subterranean economy.

THE UNITED STATES, TOO, OFFERS INCENTIVES

One is frequently made aware of incentives offered to investors in lesser-developed countries or in some hard-core unemployment area. Though less publicized, in no way less attractive are some offered to foreign investors right in the heart of the main industrial areas of the United States.

Before Volkswagen set up a car and pick-up assembly plant in 1978 in Pennsylvania, investing over $250 million and employing 5500 people, some forty states courted them. Pennsylvania won by offering what is, in effect, a series of heavily subsidized loans and outright grants, including a $40 million loan, repayable over thirty years. Interest was set at 1.75 percent during the first twenty years, which is not bad when annual inflation runs at well over 10 percent. Volkswagen also received a $10 million state bond issue, another $6 million loan at 8.5 percent interest, a $3.8 million grant towards the cost of training staff, and a five-year property tax abatement, as well as other important incentives.

If the Volkswagen accounts are to show the full advantages of the activities of this U.S. plant, the company will have to separate its income from financial and tax advantages from other operating activities. Figures presented in this way would carry more meaning than the conventional ones and would show in some detail how the U.S. government positively encourages preferential tax avoidance in ways not unique to either Pennsylvania or Volkswagen.[11]

HOW COMPANIES USE INCENTIVE SCHEMES—A CASE STUDY

Unless they really have to, multinational corporations rarely publicize the extent of the tax benefits they receive from their host. When governments and such bodies as the U.S. Securities and Exchange Commission increase the pressure on corporations seeking to raise new capital for full disclosure, a more detailed description of the benefits offered may be expected. A revealing example was the placing memorandum of a shipping company, in the early 1970s, which told the public that "outright governmental grants of approximately $11,336,000 have been obtained leaving a balance of $4,428,000 to be financed by mortgages." It goes on to describe an arrangement which "is expected to provide [the company] with cash of $23 million in 1972 which is to be retained, provided the expected tax benefits are realized. Inland Revenue has issued a non-binding advice agreeing in principle to such benefits." Later, the existence of partnership agreements is disclosed, which

> . . . are to provide for the outside partners to obtain the benefit of depreciation for tax purposes on the reefers owned by such partnerships. It is contemplated that in return the partnership will receive from the outside partners net expenses of approximately $3.9 million in 1972 and $6.5 million in 1973. Such monies will remain in the partnerships upon the mandatory retirement of the outside partners after three years unless the outside partners have not been able to obtain the agreed tax benefits.

In another connection it is revealed that "application has been made to the Government for an Investment Grant equal to approximately $6 million, which, if granted, will complete the financing of this vessel."

Finally, it is learned that the company

> . . . has a carry forward loss for tax purposes of approximately $7,500,000 as at December 31, 1971, which loss is primarily due to the double depreciation deduction. [The company] is still within the tax

benefit period with respect to its income from its first eight refrigerated ships which were granted 'approved' status as described above.

Much can be learned from financial statements and the information included therein. However, without careful study of the data available, mistaken conclusions can easily be reached. Investment in and construction of modern shipping fleets in the West were made possible by very advantageous investment grants, subsidized funding, and other incentives. Those entrepreneurs who can, avoid making their government deals public. Private capitalists who do not share ownership in their business with other shareholders rarely publish their financial statements. One never knew precisely, for instance, how much the late Howard Hughes or J. Paul Getty were worth or how much income tax, if any, they paid. There is no data available on the net worth or tax liability of the Hunt family (even after they failed to corner the silver market) or of Daniel Ludwig, probably the wealthiest American alive today. Something out of the ordinary, usually financial trouble such as insolvency or the threat of it, must occur before outsiders can gain some notion of the affairs of such private persons.

AND A CASE THAT SOURED

The financial crisis of Hilmar Reksten, a Norwegian shipping magnate, came to light in 1975. It was discovered that he had put a substantial part of his oil-carrying VLCCs (Very Large Crude [Oil] Carriers) into mothballs for the duration of the recession in the oil cargo business. He planned to keep them in the Norwegian fjords until demand increased again.

When he died in the summer of 1980, Mr. Reksten owed several hundred million dollars and was considered insolvent. But many creditors suspect that he left large assets salted away, safe from the Norwegian government and other prying eyes.

It had long been suspected but not proved that Mr. Reksten had an interest in a Liberian entity called Palmerston Holdings. This, in turn, owned one-half of a company called Anglo-Nordic Shipping, registered in Bermuda. In the early fall of 1979, Anglo-Nordic sold eight bulk carriers to Euro-Canadian Ship Holdings.

During his 1979 trial in Bergen on tax and currency charges, Mr. Reksten was accused of channeling millions of dollars to tax haven companies abroad, by means of pro forma deals. He denied ownership of the overseas companies but admitted operating them through management agreements. The prosecution could not prove ownership and the court acquitted him of the graver charges of tax fraud and currency violations. But subsequently, the tax authorities assessed him for over $120 million in back taxes on monies accrued to him from deals mentioned in the trial or on which, in the ordinary course of business, there was a statute of limitations. These taxes, like the late Mr. Reksten's other debts, have not been paid to date.

A second big creditor is the Akers Shipbuilding Group, to which Mr. Reksten's estate owes $40 to $50 million. They are still looking for a hidden Reksten stockpile. In the course of their search, they sighted another mystery company, registered in Panama and with ownership unknown. It is called Iceland Shipping, and in 1975 it bought, for $20 million, some $60 million of Mr. Reksten's debts to four international shipping lines from Norway, Canada, Britain, and Japan. The creditors could have either sued him, declared him bankrupt and lost their $60 million, or cut their losses through the Iceland Shipping offer. Not surprisingly, it is suspected that the owner of this phantom company was the late Mr. Reksten himself.*

The full details of the activities of Mr. Reksten may never come to light but some of the information offers a glimpse of how the multinational subterranean economy works.

WHAT HAPPENS TO SUBTERRANEAN FUNDS?

Much publicity has been given in recent years to sophisticated schemes involving tax havens and how self-made and well-established millionaires who were sharp enough enjoyed what the media call tax evasion one-upmanship. A wealthy individual may search for a tax haven in a rather sleepy, possibly economically backward country with a stable

* Early in 1980, members of the Reksten family attempted to close the official investigations by offering, as compensation to the creditors, some $40 million which had previously been hidden far away from the clutches of the Norwegian authorities.

government, often with an attractive subtropical or tropical climate, not necessarily close to anywhere.

The cruder, less wealthy entrepreneur has less interest, patience, time, or fear of the authorities. He may decide to try tax evasion without availing himself of the relatively expensive mechanism of the tax haven.

All the new notoriety about shelters and havens certainly influences many people who think that, in today's seemingly egalitarian society, anything the big nobs can do they can do, too. They opt to lessen their tax burden in ways that may be formally illegal but are no more damaging to the economy, in fact, than those practiced by investors in tax havens.

Where do the earners of undeclared income deposit their funds and how do they spend them? There is some evidence to show that proceeds of subterranean earnings are not applied like those from the overt economy. Although more undeclared funds are being laundered and then invested through financial institutions just like fully recorded income, other subterranean income is tucked away under pillows or mattresses all over the world. Still other underground funds are put in numbered foreign bank accounts, often but certainly not always in tax havens.

To a large extent, the decision about how to treat subterranean funds depends on the danger and risk the owners feel they are exposing themselves to and on the amounts at their disposal. The hidden income of moonlighters is usually limited. They may mix it with the reported money in their bank accounts or, more probably, just keep more cash in their pocketbooks. More often than not, they use it and simply improve their standard of living.

Capital deposited in the United States with a Cayman Islands bank, a Swiss bank, or with other financial institutions, is different in two significant respects: it is usually rather larger in amount, and the owner does not expect to use it in the short term but regards it as a long-term reserve.

A certain degree of risk is attached to these capital deposits. Whether they deposit them in their name, under a phoney identity, or in a numbered account, their owner rarely checks, on a daily, weekly, or monthly basis, the transactions made on the account. They usually extend discretionary investment authority to the bank manager. As seldom as once every year or two will they call at the branch where the funds are deposited and attempt, rather nervously, to inspect in an hour or so the changes in the account over the past year. These remote controls may prove to be risky. In the 1960s and 1970s, several small- and medium-size banks in Switzerland went into voluntary or involuntary liquidation. In these cases, the depositors of undeclared funds had less recourse than others to wage claims or to try to prove carelessness on the part of the bankers.

"I don't know the reason for sure but, whenever we organize a convention, the participants, whether they come from Latin America, South Africa, Israel, or the Arab countries stop over in Switzerland on their way in or out," commented the organizer of a worldwide meeting of international fiscal and tax consultants not long ago. "And it doesn't matter whether the conference is held in Madrid, Copenhagen, or London." For the probably increasing number of Europeans with secret accounts in Basel, Berne, or Biel, hopping over to Switzerland for a day or two is even easier and can be done more discreetly.

Other recipients of underground funds try their luck in investments. But if these are made outside the country of domicile it is very difficult to follow trends and growth or monitor what actually happens to them. Many such funds are in offshore holdings. Most people who put money in these properties believe that their earnings are totally or almost totally tax free. What they do not realize until it is too late is that these holdings are usually not seriously regulated and that their managers are not accountable to anyone for their decisions. As a substantial amount of capital invested in offshore business is income on which taxes have been avoided or evaded, owners of such properties have little chance of redress when the bubble bursts.

The most famous case of an offshore fund capsizing was that of IOS, during the late 1960s. For a short time, some of those who invested were paper millionaires. A friend told me he was, briefly, "worth" $17 million! As a large number of those suffering losses were members of the subterranean economy, there was nothing for it but for them to bite their lips and philosophize about their money being "easy come, easy go." It is difficult to attain investment security by remote control.

Still, it would appear that investors have not learned from the IOS debacle. They sign up for new programs offered and new investments in groups such as Leveraged Capital Holdings N.V. of Curaçao, the board of which is composed of prestigious European gentlemen with aristocratic names and which has put most of its assets into companies with a somewhat mysterious sound, such as Huygens Investment, Sorus Fund N.V., and Grotius Investment Corporation, all domiciled in offshore bases such as Bermuda, the Bahamas, and so on. These groups do not readily provide the detailed financial statements of their affiliates. When the requesting party insists on having the information, he or she discovers that the amount of disclosure the financial statements provide is far below the standards adopted by regularized investment groups.

REFERENCES

1. "Finding Shelter from the Storm—The Loud Proud Cry: 'We've Never Paid a Dime in Taxes,' " *Time,* September 1, 1980, p. 49.
2. See also "Regan the Inventive," *The Economist,* December 20, 1980.
3. See also Tony Doggart and Caroline Woute, *Tax Havens and Offshore Funds,* The Economist Intelligence Unit, London, 1971, p. 7.
4. See also M. A. Wisselink, "Methods of International Tax Avoidance," in *International Tax Avoidance,* a Study by the Rotterdam Institute for Fiscal Studies, Erasmus University, Rotterdam, 1979.
5. Grundy's *Tax Havens, A World Survey,* Sweet & Maxwell, London, Matthew Bender, New York, 1972.
6. *The Economist,* September 5, 1980, p. 6.
7. H. J. Browning, O.B.E., *They Didn't Declare It,* George G. Harrap, London, 1967.
8. See also "Financial Report," *The Economist,* December 11, 1980.
9. See also Christopher Tugendhat, *The Multinationals,* Eyre & Spottiswoode, London, 1971, p. 138.
10. "Why Are We Waiting?" *The Economist,* November 15, 1980, p. 25.
11. "Investing in the U.S.," survey in *The Economist,* October 25, 1980, p. 19.

11

THE SUBTERRANEAN ECONOMY IN THE UNITED STATES

One cannot reasonably quarrel with the official statistics which say that, in 1978, 89,899,669 persons submitted returns to the U.S. Internal Revenue Service, reporting an adjusted gross income less deficit of $1,304,188,847,000 or that this was an increase of 3,225,029 tax returns in one year.[1] The number of reports for 1980 increased to 93,143,000. So much for the measured economy of the United States.

The unmeasured part can only be estimated. Some 20 million Americans? With incomes of $175 billion? $250 billion? $600 billion? There are those who estimate that 5 million Americans[2] who are legally obliged to do so, in fact do not pay any taxes; their aggregate income may be over $300 billion and taxes thereon over $50 billion. Others believe that the figures involved might be higher. It is impossible to compute the figure scientifically and there is little point in taking issue with *Fortune* on this question. But their and other estimates of unrecorded activities indicate that almost everybody except the official government organs lives in daily contact with the subterranean economy; for instance, possibly one-quarter of the people working in the city of New York either moonlight or have another form of income on which they do not pay the full taxes due.

Some of the official statistics published in the United States appear, at best, questionable. The Bureau of Labor Statistics of the U.S. Department of Labor, for instance, published a paper in January 1981,[3] indicating that nearly one in twenty workers held more than one job during the survey week in May 1979. According to this study, the number of moonlighters in the United States has grown since 1969 at about the same rate as the total work force. Most indications from other sources, although perhaps not scientifically supported by figures, are that the number of moonlighters is considerably larger and that their ranks are swelling faster than those of the total work force. (See also Chapter 7, p. 60.)

However, no matter how inaccurate the statistics, when they are examined closely, the Report of the Internal Revenue Service read thoroughly, or some of the official presentations of senior treasury staff listened to, the size of the undeclared economy is seen to be awesome. Even a sensible guesstimate based on the conservative report acknowledges that, in 1976, the covert economy of the United States of America was approximately one-tenth of the surface economy.

Some idea of how far the U.S. government is from a true evaluation of the size of the subterranean economy or from determining the main obstacles the Internal Revenue Service should aim to overcome in an effort to improve compliance can be gathered from a representation made to Congress in March 1980.[4] Upon reading the full presentation, which is over 150 pages long, the reader is led to suspect that the seemingly firm figures offered by the then commissioner of Internal Revenue, Jerome Kurtz, as to the extent of various types of unreported income in fact have a less-than-solid basis; perhaps, he or she will wonder, they are actually something between a muddled guesstimate and a wild speculation, as, indeed, are many of the official data published in both the United States and other democracies. It is an unfortunate human weakness that it is far easier to understand what we can see than what isn't there. (This may be one reason why Americans find figures so comforting.) Because they are more accustomed to senior tax officers giving vague, general outlines of their subterranean economy, Europeans are often impressed by what seems to be the precision of the statements made before Congress by American experts. Queries do arise, however, when we try to find out how they arrived at their computations and when we decipher their measurements, the loopholes and conceptual errors about modes of behavior and spending habits become quite clear. It is possible that the figures published by the

American tax authorities represent minimal amounts and that, in fact, the real totals could be substantially higher. The number of tax returns for 1980 exceeded the close to 84 million votes cast in the Presidential elections of November 1980 by close to 11 percent!*

During earlier hearings, Allen Voss[5] conceded that "the extent and makeup of the subterranean economy are unknown. We have estimates of $100 billion to $200 billion (income) a year. . . . " But, after this acknowledgement of nonknowledge, Mr. Voss goes on to say that "we do know, on the basis of our own work, that the nonfiler portion of the subterranean economy in 1972 involved about five million nonfilers who received about $30 billion in taxable income and owed about $2 billion in Federal income taxes," most of whom the Internal Revenue Service did not pursue because of limited resources. One point was reiterated throughout the hearings: the pace of growth of the covert economy was quite rapid during the 1970s and is continuing so, while the official economy is barely increasing.

Whatever the figures are, and they will never be precisely determined, it can safely be stated that the total productivity of the subterranean economy of the United States is larger than the gross national product of Canada or California. Similarly, the size of the British subterranean economy is larger than the gross national product of the Republic of Ireland and, presumably, than that of Royal Kingdom of Denmark.

The subterranean economy of Canada, like many other aspects of its economy, resembles that of America although Canadian evaders are, perhaps, more reticent than their American counterparts. On the other hand, tax avoidance, as in the United States, has become big business in Canada. It has become popular with hundreds of thousands of ordinary income earners and is no longer the prerogative of the rich. Tax avoidance consultants, including lawyers, accountants, and financial institutions, are carrying on a thriving business.

Avoidance schemes in Canada are more liberal and more generally acceptable than in America. They range from

---

* Knowing that the number of those participating in the presidential elections of November 1980 was just over 50 percent of eligible voters, the number of those taxable who have not filed any returns could easily be many millions more than the Internal Revenue Service says.

deducting private school expenses and flying lessons to looking after the requirements of one's mistress. No wonder that, in light of the numerous legitimate avoidance mechanisms, one Canadian school of thought regards evasion as unwise and unnecessary.

Others believe that, even so, it is increasing at a substantial rate, that it is popular in the outlying states and territories, but also common in the more populated metropolitan areas. A liberal M.P., Mr. Donald Johnston,[6] believes that tax morality has declined astonishingly in recent years, possibly because people are unhappy about the way in which the government spends the taxes or possibly because they feel the system is inequitable. In Newfoundland, less attention is paid to the niceties of the code than in, say, Ontario. The locals there tend to ignore Ottawa. Barter and unrecorded exchange of farming, fishing, and forestry commodities is rarely an audit trail the authorities can pick up.[7]

If the estimated size of the unrecorded economies of the United States, Canada, and the Common Market are added up, their production and income is probably comparable in size to that of the United Kingdom or France: a vast but unorganized economic power and, to date, not reckoned with.

HOW THE FEDERAL BUDGET SPILLED OVER

Many critics of the subterranean economy spend too little time trying to hold back the runaway growth of the federal budget. There are no popular publications to indicate how government service has improved since, say, 1950. Yet, in current dollar terms, the federal budget of the United States grew from $66.7 billion in 1950 to $153.1 billion in 1960. It more than doubled again by 1970, reaching $338 billion, doubled once again by 1977, and will probably reach $670 billion in 1980. In other words, over thirty years it has grown thirteen times, in current value terms.

Most of the financing of this budget came from income taxes, the largest single source being taxes on individual income, which, since the end of the 1960s, has been twice as large as any other source of federal revenue. While individual income tax was less than one-third of total tax revenue in 1950, amounting to $16.5 billion, or 32.4 percent, it has, since the mid-1970s, contributed over 43 percent of total taxes, reaching

$186 billion by 1977 and $230 billion by 1980—an increase of 1500 percent in three decades.

The proportion of corporate tax to total internal revenue has been lessening. Corporate income as a percentage of total income earned in the United States has remained relatively constant over the past twenty years. But the corporate contribution to taxes paid, which amounted in 1958 to 25.2 percent of federal revenue, had dropped to 15 percent by 1973.[8]

Over this period, the official gross national product increased from $286 billion (in 1950) to just over $2.5 trillion, or about 900 percent.[9] In the same period, personal income per capita increased from $1490 to approximately $9250; 600 percent! Direct federal, state, and local taxes grew during these thirty years from $109 per capita in 1950 to $859, or 800 percent. Inflation over the same period was 258 percent.

Government controls; tax regulations; the maintenance of law and order; the welfare state; the responsibilities of the administration for health, education, and welfare; and, often, an enormous defense budget have led democratic government to intervene in the day-to-day life of the economy to an extent unprecedented, even in the authoritarian countries. Walter E. Williams of the SmithKline Corporation cites the tax licensing laws, which, in most cities of the United States, are among the most flagrant examples of monopoly and collusion. Whereas in the 1920s a poor, industrious immigrant in New York City could buy a used car, paint "taxi" on it, and be in business, today's poor New Yorker must have not only a car but also $60,000 for a tax license. In addition, the bureaucracy he or she will encounter before getting a license is often frustrating. No wonder many, mostly blacks and Hispanics, have ignored the city-granted monopoly and entered a "gypsy" taxi industry, where they earn an honest, hard, albeit illegal, living.

Government surveillance and interference increases the human urge for privacy and causes more secretiveness. In the course of this increased presence, an action such as an exchange of valuable presents between cousins or friendly services mutually rendered but not billed by doctor and attorney, which, until a generation ago, was an innocent, private transaction, has come to be questioned as a criminal act. Official definitions of income can be vague; try, for instance, to define when growing your own vegetables is taxable. When and what overtime is taxable? It is often difficult to define the difference between what is legal and legitimate and what is not. Perks which may be acceptable in some countries are regarded as theft in others, while clever tax planning consultants spend huge funds and much time designing novel perks to offset the impact of new or more taxation. At every level of the economic hierarchy, there are members of the subterranean economy. Their underground activities are neither haphazard nor the result of a fluke.[10]

The subterranean economy today is complementary to the actions of the state, the politicians, and the civil servants who operate it. Complex interaction between them swings and influences the trends of growth of the hidden part of the economy.

AN UNWIELDY BUREAUCRACY FOSTERS THE UNMEASURED ECONOMY

Few people doubt that the United States of America is physically and economically the strongest country in the world. Soul-searching has, for years, been a favorite American pastime. It intensified in the 1970s, in the wake of Vietnam, Watergate, and the fall of President Nixon. Most of it has had to do in recent years with what went wrong, where and when?

In a speech made in the fall of 1979 by a senior American banker, Joseph J. Pinola, to the California Savings & Loan League,[11] he said that America had changed from being a nation which encouraged productivity to one in which it was penalized; U.S. government regulation had set itself the highly laudable goal of helping the consumer but at the expense of the producer, whether he produced goods or capital and savings for investment. Inflationary paper profits were unfairly taxed. The result was that, at 5 percent, the U.S. rate of personal savings was the lowest in the industrialized world. Mr. Pinola highlighted the role of government in this shift of emphasis with some examples. He showed that federal government regulatory agency budgets have doubled over a few years; that some companies spend more laborhours on government paperwork than on their own projects; and that the cost of regulation in 1976 equalled more than 8 percent of the GNP. In 1979, government-introduced regulatory laws were estimated to have cost the average family of four over $4000.

He also said that in a typical day 242 congressional committees and subcommittees meet in Washington for law-enactment purposes.

What Mr. Pinola said was not new. Little has been done in recent years to make profit and investment enticing in the United States, nor did his words seem to have impressed the then administration with any need to improve the situation.

Modern documentation has overflown many dams, and there are those who fear it will swamp us all. The swell is so great, there appears to be no immediate way in which to control it. In recent years, Americans produced 72 billion documents annually. There are approximately 18,000 (!) papers for every white-collar worker in the United States, which, in effect, means keeping more than 300 billion records, vouchers, and other documents on file. The cost of producing documents has also increased rapidly: producing a regular business letter can easily set you back $8; trying to locate one misfiled document can amount to more than $60. And firms mislay anywhere between 1 and 5 percent of their records.[12]

Early in 1980, a considerable amount of publicity was given to Donald Lambro's book.[13] The blurbs, alone, were an interesting expression of current attitudes, dissatisfaction with federal handling of inflation, and a general feeling of government waste, mismanagement, and muddle. Alongside the suspicion of bumbling, the attitude of "It is not really worth paying taxes; you are a sucker if you do" is gradually becoming widespread and a popular subject for debate at all levels in the media.

JUST TO KNOW THE TAX LAW IS A FULL-TIME JOB

In the United States of America, a country proud of its pluralistic heritage and trust in free enterprise, the amount of time and money required when encountering the tax system and other regulatory authorities is often exasperating.*

The complexity, range, and number of tax reports required of a new, young sole proprietor of a business being set up in the city of New York, for instance, can easily lead him or her to

---

* A brief description of the unwieldy, inhuman form of tax language is given in Chapter 5, pp. 41–42.

despair.* Assuming the owner lives in any one of the five boroughs, he or she is liable for no less than twenty(!) different taxes or statements, and if two or more staff are employed, he or she must file at least thirty-seven separate tax reports annually. Of these, six are with the city, seventeen with the federal authorities, and the remaining fourteen with the state authorities. If, in addition to business involvements, he or she lives or owns property in or carries on business away from New York City, the number of reports inevitably multiplies. While the tax burden is obviously considerable, the indirect cost of filing all these documents, that is, the time and money needed to prepare the material demanded by the various authorities for the greatest possible benefit of the assess, is less clearly realized and more difficult to quantify.

Partnerships and corporations are expected to report similarly and, as their business grows in size, more and more legions of staff must be employed, aided by outside consultants. Some fill out federal and other forms while the rest are kept busy seeking legitimate ways to reduce the company's tax burden. Together, they consume an increasing part of the company's overhead.

The number of taxes payable and, even more, the number of forms the average businessperson must fill in regularly varies from state to state. But, even in the states with the least bureaucracy, the number is growing and acts as a powerful disincentive to initiative and to the growth of fully tax-observing free enterprise.

Quite obviously, the various tax laws and instructions have grown to be too cumbersome for the average American or, for that matter, for the citizens of most welfare states.

It is evident, from a study published in March 1980,[14] that it is difficult or complicated to prepare one's own tax returns and that one might lose by doing it oneself. According to the questionnaire on which this survey was based, 44 million Americans had someone else prepare their 1978 tax returns for them. Over 33 million of them employed a lawyer, accountant, or commercial tax firm. Most explained their request for help by saying that the "forms were too complicated," that they

---

* See the Appendix, which sets out the schedule of almost all the tax forms that sole proprietorships operating in New York City must consider filing.

were "afraid they might make mistakes" and thought that, by using such aid, they "hoped to save some (tax money)."

Tax laws are the only ones which today affect virtually all Americans in their everyday life. Most of them believe it advisable to retain specialist know-how to help them stay within the law and minimize their tax liability.

INFLATION INCREASES YOUR INCOME TAX LIABILITY

It is common knowledge that inflation hurts the economy in many ways, but its influence on the tax rates paid by individuals was underestimated until the 1970s. The problem became quite acute throughout the free democracies as inflation rose from a general annual 1 to 4 percent in the 1960s to 6 to 20 percent in the 1970s. As a result, a single individual, for example, whose money income rose from $15,000 in 1978 to $16,200 in 1979 (an 8 percent increase) would have, in effect, experienced a 1 percent drop in real income. If 1978 tax schedules had remained in effect in 1979, this individual's tax liability would have increased and his or her disposable income dropped still further. There were tax adjustments in 1979 which reduced but did not, for most people, eliminate the effect of this bracket creep. In the past thirty years, although personal income tax reductions have periodically been legislated, inflation more than offset these cuts, with the net effect of a gradual increase in the real taxation of individuals. These increases were made heavier by a relatively fast rise in both social security and state and local taxes. So, while statistics do not always fully disclose economic funds, they still are, when properly compiled, indicative of trends and changes. Relative to the total disclosed personal income, they rose from approximately 11 percent in 1950 to 15 percent in 1965 and to about 23 percent in 1980. In part, this is a result of congressional legislation, but in part it is a result of the tax-bracket creep inevitable during periods of inflation. It has the effect of enlarging the drop in real after tax income.[15]

The tax reduction program proposed by President Reagan in February 1981 (and approved by Congress in July 1981) which would gradually reduce direct taxes during the coming few years, will, perhaps, help strengthen his immediate popularity, but it is doubtful whether it will persuade those with unmeasured income to rejoin the declared economy.

THERE ARE LEGITIMATE WAYS TO AVOID TAXES

It is difficult to assess just how much the high marginal tax rates in the United States or in western Europe deter income earners from declaring their income. One thing becomes clear when analyzing published statistics: according to the spirit of the law, many who reach high incomes and would be liable for high tax rates succeed, through legitimate avoidance, in paying far less taxes. In many cases, the average tax the wealthy pay on their income is lower than that of middle-class earners.[16]

Accordingly, in 1976, of those earning between $50,000 and $100,000 on an "adjusted gross income plus preferences" base, 45.3 percent averaged an effective tax rate of over 25 percent. Compared to these, about 22.7 percent of those earning over $200,000 on the same basis were liable for an amount of taxes which represented less than 25 percent of their income.[17]

There are numerous ways in which to reduce taxes on income through deductions and credits. These include, to name a few of the major items:

- Investment credits
- Foreign tax credits
- Interest deductions
- Medical deductions
- Casualty loss deductions
- Contributions deductions
- Taxes paid deductions

And there are any number of other legitimate avoidance opportunities intended as such, as well as unintentional loopholes.

HOW MUCH IN TAXES DOES THE INTERNAL REVENUE SERVICE THINK IT FAILS TO COLLECT?

Statistics also show that unreported income accruing to people who do not file any returns ranges from $27.5 billion to $64.1 billion. The result, according to the Report of the Internal Revenue Service, was that, in 1978, the federal government may have lost about 15 percent of personal income tax due.

Unreported income from legal sources was about three times more than that from illegal ones. Missing tax was estimated at between $25.9 billion and $29.1 billion, compared with $142 billion personal income taxes actually paid. Between $6.3 billion and $8.8 billion of the missing tax had its source in criminal activity.

While the difference between the minimum and maximum figure is substantial, skeptics may ask how the subterranean economy can be so measured and yet these evaders persist in their nonreporting habits? Not contested is the statement of Internal Revenue Service Commissioner Jerome Kurtz[18] that reporting is more accurate when incomes are subject to tax deductions at source, such as in the case of salaried workers. It is also acceptable that the tax returns are relatively accurate when there are reporting requirements as, for instance, with dividends and interest payments.

The actual condensed tables of illegal types of income show that total unrecorded income in 1976 was as follows:

	Billions
Illegal drugs	$16.2 – 23.6
Bookmaking	4.0 – 5.0
Numbers	2.4 – 3.0
Other gambling	1.6 – 2.0
Prostitution	1.1 – 1.6
Total	$25.3 – 35.2

Many members of the public were shocked when, following a spate of disclosures of how some of the most respectable American corporations participated in giving kickbacks to foreign agents, Congress passed the Foreign Corrupt Practices Act into law. Others remembered that kickbacks have a tendency to stay glued to the payer. There was loud talk of the recent upsurge in the subterranean economy. Then, in July 1979, the comptroller general, in a report to the U.S. Congress, presented a 114-page analysis,[19] which was noted in the general press. A report such as this had become inevitable after all the publicity, and it made a serious pitch to strengthen the Internal Revenue Service by upgrading its methods of work. It indicates that the Internal Revenue Service needs to give more attention to the problem of people who do not file income tax returns by:

- studying the make-up of the nonfiling population and drawing conclusions, and
- pursuing nonfilers more energetically and expanding their efforts to catch them.

The report commences by stating that some 87 billion taxpayers filed individual federal income tax returns in 1978, compared with some 68 million in 1972; in other words, in six years the number of filings increased by approximately 27 percent. Total gross tax collections amounted to $213 billion. All this involves an overwhelming amount of paperwork, which even a large organization like the Internal Revenue Service finds difficult to process. Mr. Richard L. Fogel, the associate director general, Government Division,[20] stated that the Internal Revenue Service could not afford to authenticate more than 54 percent of the documents it received for 1977. Later, discussing the use of magnetic media, Mr. Fogel said that the number of documents presented in this form has risen from 48 million in 1968 to about 435 million for 1978, or 87 percent of the 501 million total! He called the practitioners of tax avoision "unfair" and cited the words of Oliver Wendell Holmes, engraved in stone above the main entrance to the building of Internal Revenue Service National Headquarters in Washington, D.C.: "Taxes are what we pay for a civilized society." He made a seemingly genetic distinction between the common American, burdened with duties, and the elite corps of civil servants. He forgot that when Mr. Holmes made his admirable statement, marginal tax rates were lower than 10 percent, the number of Americans required to comply was probably fewer than 10 million, and the government budget was in the general range of 10 percent of the gross national product. It is presumptuous of Mr. Fogel to suggest that Oliver Wendell Holmes would say the same in this era of imperial bureaucracy.

Mr. Donald Lubick, assistant secretary to the U.S. Treasury, was less general in scope and more precise on the subject when, in September 1979, he told a Senate subcommittee that almost half of 50,000 independent contractors checked by the

Internal Revenue Service had not reported any income for tax purposes; over 60 percent had paid no social security taxes.[21]

As it is questionable whether the Internal Revenue Service is able to locate all the contractors who assess their own income and pay tax estimates quarterly, he may even have been overly optimistic.

WHY THE DISENCHANTMENT WITH THE TAX SYSTEM?

It is considerably simpler to test sample the extent of general disappointment with the tax system than to quantify the size of the hidden economy in any methodical way. In the United States, such a statistical study[22] done in the late spring of 1979 has shown that, while one-half of those questioned believed that controlling inflation was the most urgent task facing the administration, well over one-third of those questioned believed that "making the tax system fairer," "lowering income taxes," "simplifying income tax returns," and "lowering social security taxes" were of top urgency. Early in 1978, before inflation reached a two-digit figure, worry about the fairness and size of taxes seemed to be the most acute problem for those sampled. According to these questionnaires, it is quite clear that a sizable part of the American public has, for at least some years, been truly exasperated by the amount of taxes it has had to pay. Close to two-thirds of those asked said that the federal income tax they had to pay was either "somewhat high" or "excessively high," while less than a quarter believed that taxes are "about right." In other words, a ratio of close to three to one. About one-tenth did not pay taxes and therefore were not really involved.

To check these results, those interviewed were asked to describe their feelings as to the fairness of the tax system. Approximately the same ratio of two in three answered that the income tax system was either "somewhat" or "quite" unfair.

One of the greatest challenges to which Ronald Reagan was committed, during his election campaign, was the reduction of federal taxes. His success at the end of July 1981, when Congress resolved to cut taxes by 25 percent over a period of three years, was, possibly, one of the highlights of his first year in the White House. But a tax cut has a greater impact on the taxpayers if it increases their trust in the economy, and businesspeople on Wall Street were, like many other Americans, worried by the fact that there was no parallel cut in government expenditure; they felt that this would lead to increased deficit financing. It would be unproductive to try to foretell to what extent members of the unrecorded economy will now choose to join the open economy.

Earlier, a study conducted by the Roper Organization, the results of which were published in 1979,[23] established that well over half of those asked believe that taxes can be cut by one-third, in accordance with the Kemp-Roth bill,* without reducing the level of government services. It is not surprising that well over two-thirds, nearly three in four, of those questioned in May 1978 were in favor of the Kemp-Roth bill.

Statisticians and other surveyors of public opinion concur that no research techniques have been developed that could quantify the extent of tax avoidance and/or cheating.** Still, while exploring tax diversion, the Roper Study did find, in May 1978, "considerable tax avoidance, [and] a strong conviction that cheating is widespread." Some 13 percent of those sampled at the time acknowledged that they had participated in some barter transactions and some 14 percent acknowledged that they had agreed at least once during the year to a salesman's request to pay in cash, rather than by check, credit card, or charge account.

Well over a quarter of those asked (27 percent) admitted that they had been less than absolutely honest in completing their 1978 tax returns; 9.1 percent said they had stretched the truth a little to enable them to pay fewer taxes for that year.[24]

Answers to other questions about the subterranean economy were more conceptual. It would appear that the people questioned believed that some 7 percent of those who should file income tax returns do not do so; of those who do file, well

---

* Named after Republican Congressman Jack Kemp of New York and Republican Senator William Roth of Delaware, who proposed in 1978 that a law be introduced that would cut federal income taxes by one-third over a three-year period.

** *The Third Annual Tax Study,* commissioned by H & R Block and carried out by the Roper Organization, Inc., July 1979, pp. 61–62. "We were under no illusions . . . about the accuracy of the results obtained, nor their comprehensiveness. The elements of illegality . . . would bias responses to certain kinds of questions."

over 20 percent report at least 20 percent less taxable income than they really have. The report went on to estimate that the number of Americans who claim at least $1000 more tax-deductible expenses than they are actually entitled to reached 40 percent.

The study summarizes this group of questions by establishing that well over two-thirds of those who answered believe that cheating the Internal Revenue Service is either fairly or very common. It is most frequent among executives and professionals, the self-employed, and those angry about taxes.

And, on to a second study.

In spite of the very low number actually prosecuted and sent to jail (see p. 44), the majority of Americans believe that "most people who think about cheating decide not to, because they have heard how the government punishes tax cheaters."[25]

It is impossible to ascertain whether those questioned were fully candid or giving lip service to the system or whatever.

The Internal Revenue Service developed its compliance system using the psychological stimulus of fear. The evidence of tax protest today, ranging from legitimate demonstrations like those in California in 1978 concerning Proposition 13 to the more spontaneous ones have grown very rapidly in recent years, and there are indications of the increased awareness by the Internal Revenue Service of just how strong opposition to the tax system is.

There appears to be an increased level of tolerance of tax evasion in the United States. Over 40 percent of those asked, for instance, did not disagree with the statement that "people who disagree with how federal tax is spent should have a right to refuse to pay some of their taxes," and over a quarter of those asked did not disagree with the statement that "people who think a tax is illegal or unconstitutional should not be punished for refusing to pay the tax." From the answers to all questions related to this subject, it was clear that in 1979 tax cheating was considered less serious than it had been in the mid-1960s.

The more liberal approach to evasion was also expressed in the answers to another group of questions. Compared to some 35.5 percent of those asked in 1966, over 44 percent believed in 1979 that "almost every taxpayer cheats a little." A climb of one-quarter. Alongside this, a lighter, more lenient attitude to petty cheating was noticeable: whereas close to one-third of those asked in 1966 had recommended that small cheaters should be heavily fined, jailed, or both, in 1979 the number expressing this opinion dropped to just over 8 percent. There was more tolerance of large-scale tax cheaters, as well. The proportion recommending a jail term remained virtually unchanged, at just over a quarter of those sampled, but the percentage proposing heavy fines dropped from almost 52 percent to 45.4 percent; the fines recommended were lighter, and those satisfied with simply having the evaders pay the taxes owed (with interest or without) increased from over 18 percent to over 28 percent.

It is also of some interest to note that some three-quarters of the Americans sampled would not take any action if they knew someone was cheating, unlike the Swiss, for instance, many of whom would squeal.

Summarizing the taxpayers' attitudes, the researchers suggested that, while most Americans did not see evasion as a means to their own personal protest or to expressing their dissatisfaction, almost one-half believed that tax protest served a useful purpose.

And another observation: although fewer get caught, tax cheating was classified as more serious a crime than exceeding the 55 miles per hour speed limit, but it was thought less serious than stealing the equivalent amount of cash or filing misleading claims to social security.

SO, CRIME MONEY INTERMINGLES WITH REGULAR TAX-EVADED INCOME

As long ago as around 1960, an American writer by the name of David T. Bazelon observed that one of the economic impacts income tax has is that many people think of two completely separate types of U.S. currency: before-tax money and after-tax money. Today, many in practice reject this differentiation and seek ways that will permit after-tax money to be identical with before-tax money.

The disclosures to the congressional subcommittee headed by Congressman Ben Rosenthal at the hearings of September 5 and 6, 1979, and the booklet published following these,[26] to which a series of appendices was added, place emphasis on the billions of dollars lost through moonlighting evasion, the use of cash to evade taxes, and, to a lesser extent, barter. Mention is made of crime money, but less of illicit funds generated by the illegal immigrants or the thriving unreported income of the multinational. Possibly this is because the subcommittee limited its hearings to these aspects of the unrecorded economy.

This is true, also, as far as American publications are concerned. In recent years, reference was made in the United States to the subterranean economy, and many articles appeared on the subject. They invariably omitted the same aspects as the congressional subcommittee ignored and dealt with elements comparable to those taken up in the hearings.

Publicity describing how clever notable figures in the news are in their avoidance gambits—usually free of any disparaging tone—breeds more jealousy on the part of those in lower income brackets or in some less fortunate line of work, where such perks are unavailable.

Little public attention has, however, been given to other points concerning the tax ramifications that should be made obvious and have a considerable influence on the growth of this economy: the perks, shelters, or other incentives which enable the above-average income earner and the wealthy person to reduce the tax paid to a lower rate than the average employee. Nor have come under consideration the legal methods used by large, publicly owned corporations to reduce—sometimes to insignificant rates—their provisions for tax liabilities.

The hearings addressed themselves in general to less sophisticated examples of the subterranean economy. In the booklet later published, there was one exception to the general attitude: a Mr. August Bequal, attorney at law, Washington, D.C., whose prepared statement was read to the committee. Mr. Bequal second-graded moonlighting, emphasizing that democracy was in greater danger from the power elements that break the law unpunished. Not surprisingly, he found white-collar felons and gangsters more dangerous to the state than housewives with undeclared incomes on the side.

One of the more striking facts about the institutional approach to the subterranean economy, which came to light during the hearings and should have been queried, is the time lag in the figures presented. The Internal Revenue Service and the General Accounting Office both depended on surveys and statistics relating to 1976 and even as far back as 1972! Other data referred to work carried out by the Chamber of Commerce of the United States in 1973 and concerned analyses and estimates of white-collar crime in the early 1970s. It identified:

- Bankruptcy-related frauds
- Bribery, kickbacks, and payoffs
- Computer-related crime
- Consumer fraud
- Credit card and check fraud
- Embezzlement and pilferage
- Insurance fraud
- Security theft and fraud
- Receiving stolen property schemes

Each and every one of these is a multibillion-dollar business, and it may safely be assumed that with inflation and the fading away of the old dictum that "crime doesn't pay" (sadly, another fallacy with which we grew up), their growth has mushroomed since the 1973 report was drawn up.

Only after adding hard crime—the drug trade, hijacking, prostitution, loansharking, and so on—and assessing the success of its penetration into the labor movement, Wall Street, pension funds, and other legitimate elements of the economy, can the dynamics of the independent existence of this parallel, quasi–self-controlled economy be really understood.

When one considers the measures suggested or taken by the senior executives of the various tax agencies, one may legitimately conclude, that, while some have powerful gimmicks or even short-term tactics, they do not have a seriously thought-out strategic program to reduce the size of the subterranean economy. Some of them may have despaired of getting the kind of political backup they believe they require to conduct a well-planned campaign. Others regard themselves as technicians and have no pretensions to reduce the incidence of subterranean dealings. For them, it will suffice if the pace of growth is contained while they are in office.*

SOME COMMON WAYS OF FIBBING

A favorite avoision practice is fibbing on inventories. The small businessperson learns early on that the smaller the inventory the lighter the tax liability. Misrepresenting the year-end inventory lies somewhere in the terrain between avoidance and evasion; it is certainly a way in which to reduce taxable income. Many independent auditors are aware of the habit and try to detect it at work, but few have the expertise to evaluate the degree of trickery of their client. Large corporations that avail themselves of Last In, First Out (LIFO) inventory costing need not revert to the cruder cheating methods of small businesses. But, as Daniel Halperin, deputy assistant secretary for tax policy at the Treasury Department, explained, "The current complexity in the use of LIFO effectively denies small business its benefits."[27] And a recent Internal Revenue Study indicated that inventory adjustments had been made in one-quarter of the audited firms with assets of not more than $1 million.[27]

There are those who claim that an underpricing of inventories—say at 80 percent of cost—is both careful management and good accounting practice; if it is carried out consistently, it will usually be backed up by the independent accountants. Modern computer programming caters to the wishes of management by providing full information on the movement of products and for understating inventories. The figures rise rapidly as the size of the business increases. A large shopkeeper in Chicago or New York, for example, who reports his or her firm's $3 million dollar inventory at 80 percent of cost is hiding some $600,000; at a 46 percent tax rate, he or she is "saving" over $275,000 that would otherwise have been paid as income taxes. That is a significant figure, and the frequency

* A typical example of the work of tax officers of the latter group is the "Report on the Study of Illegal Tax Protester Activities" published in March 1979 and appearing as Appendix 2 to *Subterranean or Underground Economy, Hearings before a Subcommittee of the Committee on Government Operations,* published by the U.S. Government Printing Office, Washington, D.C., 1979, pp. 144ff. The objectives of the study group were as follows: (1) to delimit the tax protest movement and gauge its effect on avoision, (2) to establish how effective are procedures to deal with tax protesters, and (3) to work out new procedures.

of such practices would indicate what a multibillion-dollar business conservative inventory valuations has become. If exposed, the businessperson will claim that declaring full value and paying the ensuing tax could have put him or her into financial straits.

As the deductible donation industry has in recent years continued to grow, new opportunities for evasion have opened up. It is increasingly common for charitable, academic, or medical institutions to be approached by the trustees of some estate or other with the offer of a grant. Enthusiastic at the prospect and delighted that there are no strings attached about the use of the donation, the directors of the institution often agree, as a gesture of their appreciation, to note receipt of a larger sum than the actual donation, some of which is then paid back to the trustees in some sort of a kickback arrangement.

Another form of avoision is the establishment of a so-called church, the "ministers" of which have a diminished tax liability. They contribute some of their income to the alleged church, which, in turn, provides their housing, car expenses, and the cost of using a "retreat" in a holiday spot.

Going one step further, imaginative entrepreneurs now enable taxpayers to become church ministers by mail. The taxpayer purchases a divinity certification and then claims exempt status.

ON THE SIZE OF THE INTERNAL REVENUE SERVICE

Still, some Americans are proud of one piece of statistical fact: the cost of operating the Internal Revenue Service successfully is relatively low; at less than .5 percent of gross revenue, it compares well even with the United Kingdom at just under 2 percent.

Unlike in Britain, where it is the employer's responsibility to deduct taxes at source from the wages of his employees based on regulations and schedules issued by the Inland Revenue, U.S. law permits employees to tell their boss how much tax to withhold from their paycheck; it is then up to the employees to report their income from all sources and send the balance of tax due to the Internal Revenue Service. If they make a genuine mistake, they have to pay interest on their tax. If they are caught cheating, they must pay tax plus interest plus a stiff fine and could face a prison term. This "honor" system has resulted in the staff of the U.S. Internal Revenue Service being approximately one-quarter the size of that in the United Kingdom. Those who believe the breakdown of the tax morality is purely an administrative problem blame the fact that evasion is thriving on the lack of Internal Revenue staff. The service has some 18,600 employees to examine its returns. Their total ranks have grown by two-thirds since 1960, to a total of 85,000 in 1980. Their pace of growth was more rapid in the 1960s. During the 1970s, the increase was a modest 17 percent. Going by the hypothesis that a businessperson puts his or her money where returns are highest, Lee Smith[28] theorized that, if the Internal Revenue Service were a business venture, its officers would long ago have increased its operating budget. He supports his contention by pointing out that the return on a marginal dollar collected runs at 600 percent, while an additional dollar invested in Internal Revenue Service auditors should yield $7 in revenue.

The average return on monies invested by the Internal Revenue Service is far higher. On a budget of $2.1 billion in 1979, it collected $460 billion, or $0.46 for every $100 collected, a very respectable result. Even the more expensive British operation at $19 for $1000 is regarded as costing a respectable and reasonable amount.

As long as it was believed that this voluntary system was operating fairly well, there was great support for it. But then, in recent years, as evasion and avoidance were suspected to be increasing, the revenue service came to the conclusion that wage earners were developing devious and imaginative ways of fiddling. It was discovered that they claimed too many deductions on the W-4 withholding forms filed with employers, ranging from dependents to mortgage interest relief. This has resulted in a new regulation requiring employers to notify the Internal Revenue Service when employees show ten deductions or more or claim total tax exemptions exceeding $200 a week on their salaries.

THE TAX CONFRONTATION GOES ON

The conflict, which inflation sharpens, between what the citizen believes his or her debts to the state to be and, on the other hand, what the authorities expect from the taxpayer raises a more important question than the mere payment of taxes. In the past generation, the point has been reached at which the state has put the taxpayer in a straitjacket. The system has become, in many ways, despotic and tyrannical. The politicians who promote it without being fully aware of its social and economic ramifications are, in the last analysis, callous and demagogic. They have been able to enact legislation with as much ease as they did by playing upon people's feelings of malice and, sometimes, envy of neighbors who seem better off but may be just more ostentatious. It was inevitable that the citizens would realize the unfairness of the system in due course and make it more difficult for the Internal Revenue Service to enforce its code.

One of the techniques of the tax protesters is to hinder the Internal Revenue Service in its work and then complain that it does not work properly. Some have become more hostile, and Internal Revenue staff are being harrassed by tax protesters and have reason to fear for their physical safety.

It is much more "in" to be a tax dodger today than it was a generation ago. As previously mentioned, in January 1980, for instance, several taxpayers went so far as to describe, openly and brazenly, on the CBS program "60 Minutes," how they left large amounts of income off their returns. Society—politicians, businesspeople, academics, artists, and artisans alike—no longer regards a white-collar criminal tax verdict as more than an occupational hazard, which certainly contributes to lessening the deterrent effect the guardians of the law may have.

There are other indications of the erosion in the prestige of the Internal Revenue Service, both empirical and anecdotal. According to Columbia University Professor of Tax Law Martin Ginsberg, sophisticated taxpayers know of the low incidence of federal audits (in 1979 only 2.24 percent of all tax returns were audited) and of their shallow approach. Therefore, they often feel free to dispense with costly tax consultations.[29]

Although the tax audit sampling system reaches only a few and is often inefficient, it does give enormous power to a group of relatively independent civil servants. Their ability to decide who should be investigated amounts to a political tool, potentially dangerous. Its misuse in the United States was described in various books published during the 1970s.*

And yet, the regulatory agencies have not been allocated the budgets and staff to assess economic activities from a multinational viewpoint or to study the tactics of those who manipulate international business finances. Therefore, they do not have the expertise needed to give them a perspective to understand the wider problems posed by the outside elements.

On the side of the public, protecting it from the dangers of an overly zealous tax-collecting corps, are the American courts. The Internal Revenue Service, increasingly nervous as it is, finds it difficult to enforce the law because American courts give protection to possible evaders. In 1980, for example, Mobil Oil was supported by the courts in its refusal to hand over payroll records to the Internal Revenue Service to help detect employee tax fiddling. And a lower court decision supported Brigham Young University in its refusal to provide a complete donor list to speed up Internal Revenue Service investigations which had detected widespread tax cheating amoung the university's wealthy contributors. The Supreme Court has refused to review a California Appeals Court ruling which the Internal Revenue Service claims could make tax avoidance as easy as apple pie. The question at issue was whether the Internal Revenue Service should be compelled, under the Freedom of Information Act, to disclose how they choose the 50,000 returns on which they carry out an intensive audit in conformity with the Taxpayer Compliance Measurement Program.

Full enforcement is a rather theoretical ideal. One fact certainly emerges: the enormity of the subterranean economy of the United States. In this age of big government and often aloof bureaucracy, the question of how to increase public and individual taxpaying motivation and acceptance of the voluntary tax system is a most difficult challenge to leadership. It should be understood that, if the Internal Revenue Service were to make every effort to collect every cent due to it, America would be much closer to being a police state. Unless,

---

* To name a few: Theodore H. White, *Breach of Faith*, Jonathan Cape, pp. 74 and 151; Woodward & Bernstein, *The Final Days*, Secker & Warburg, p. 89; William Manchester, *The Glory and the Dream*, Jospeh, pp. 604–606.

that is, the federal deficit could be reduced by a more effective tax collection method. Success or failure in reaching this objective will be one of the yardsticks for measuring the Republican administration of President Reagan.

REFERENCES

1. *1978 Statistics of Income/Individual Income Tax Return,* Internal Revenue Service Publication No. 198, April 1980, p. 1.
2. Lee Smith, "The $50 Billion that the IRS Is Not Collecting," *Fortune,* March 10, 1980.
3. "Multiple Jobholders in May, 1979," *Special Labor Force Report No. 239* by Edward S. Sekscenski, an economist in the Office of Employment Analysis, Bureau of Labor Statistics, 1979.
4. "Estimates of Income Unreported on Individual Income Tax Returns," presented by the Internal Revenue Service, Department of the Treasury at the Hearings on Public Debt Limitations before the Committee on Ways and Means, House of Representatives, March 3, 1980.
5. Hearings before the Subcommittee on Oversight of the Committee on Ways and Means, House of Representatives, on the Underground Economy, July 16, 1979, Allen R. Voss, then Director, General Government Division, General Accounting Office.
6. "Living the Deductible Life," *Canadian Business,* January 1979, pp. 33–38.
7. See also "The Underground Economy May Upset Ottawa's Plans," *Financial Post,* October 6, 1979.
8. Richard J. Barnet and Ronald E. Muller, *Global Reach, the Power of the Multinational Corporations,* Simon and Schuster, New York, 1974, p. 273.
9. Sources: *Statistical Abstract of the U.S., 1979,* plus estimates based on *Survey of Current Business.* The 1980 gross national product is based on estimates of the Department of Commerce.
10. See also Jason Ditton, Stuart Henry, Gerald Mars, and Peter Mitchell, *Policing the Hidden Economy: The Significance and Control of Fiddles,* Outer Circle Unit, London, 1979.
11. Joseph J. Pinola, chairman of the board, Western Bancorporation, addressing the California Savings & Loan League, San Francisco, September 27, 1979.
12. "Business Brief," *The Economist,* December 27, 1980, relying on research of the Yankee Group of Cambridge, Massachusetts.
13. Donald Lambro, *Fat City: How Washington Wastes Your Taxes,* Regency/Gateway, Inc, South Bend, Indiana, 1980.

14. *A General Taxpayer Opinion Survey,* prepared by Sherrie S. Aitken and Lawra Bonneville for the Office of Planning and Research, Internal Revenue Service and discussing income tax returns, mainly for 1978, by CSR Incorporated, Washington, D.C., March 1980.

15. See also Courtney Slater, "Taxes Reach Record Share of Income, Will Rise Further Under Current Laws," *Business America,* June 16, 1980, pp. 20–21.

16. See *High Income Tax Returns 1975 and 1976—A Report Emphasizing Nontaxable and Nearly Nontaxable Income Tax Returns,* The Office of Tax Analysis, U.S. Treasury Department, Washington, D.C., August 1978.

17. *Distribution of Tax Returns by Income Class and Effective Tax Rate,* Office of Income Tax Analysis, 1976, Table 5, p. 25.

18. Hearings on Subterranean or Underground Economy, Statement of Jerome Kurtz, then commissioner of Internal Revenue, before the Commerce, Consumer, and Monetary Affairs Subcommittee of the Committee on Government Operations, September 5, 1979.

19. *Who's Not Filing Income Tax Returns? IRS Needs Better Ways to Find Them and Collect Their Taxes,* Comptroller General, Washington, D.C., July 1979.

20. Richard L. Fogel, in a statement on the Subterranean Economy, before the Subcommittee, Consumer and Monetary Affairs, House Committee on Government Operations, U.S. Government Printing Office, Washington, D.C., September 6, 1979.

21. "Welcome to the Black Economy," *Time,* September 29, 1979, p. 36.

22. *The Third Annual Tax Study,* commissioned by H & R Block and carried out by the Roper Organization, Inc., H & R Block Public Affairs Department, Kansas City, Missouri, July 1979, p. 58.

23. Ibid.

24. Ibid, p. 13.

25. According to the sample taken in *A General Taxpayer Opinion Survey,* Washington, D.C., for the Office of Planning and Research of the Internal Revenue Service, Washington, D.C., March 1980.

26. *Subterranean or Underground Economy, Hearings before a Subcommittee of the Committee on Government Operations,* U.S. Government Printing Office, Washington, D.C.

27. "Little Guys Cheat on Inventory to Hide Goods, Evade Taxes," *The Wall Street Journal,* August 4, 1980.

28. Lee Smith, op. cit.

29. Ibid.

12

THE SUBTERRANEAN ECONOMY IN BRITAIN AND THE COMMON MARKET

LIKE TOPSY, AVOISION JUST KEEPS ON GROWING

To understand the growth of government presence in the national economies of western Europe, it is useful to compare general government expenditure (including transfer payments) and the gross domestic product from the mid-1950s to the mid-1970s. In the early 1950s, none of the western democracies' budgets were higher than one-third of their respective gross domestic product figures. In the three years ending in 1975, the government budgets of Sweden and the Netherlands were approximately half the gross domestic products of those countries; those of France, Italy, Belgium, West Germany, and Britain were over 40 percent and still growing. In these countries, where tax revenue is the main source of government expenditure, direct taxes continued to increase substantially in the ten years between 1965 and 1975. Thus, in Britain, direct taxes on income increased from 37 to 44 percent. In France and Italy, with their notorious tax evasion habits, direct taxes collected were considerably lower; they grew from 16 to 18 percent in France and from 18 to 22 percent in Italy.

During this period, there was little public resistance to the high tax rates included in the various governmental income projections. Budgets were regularly approved in Parliament and only rarely was there a serious call to reduce taxes.

Not all taxes were raised through legislation: part of the increase is attributable to fiscal drag. In periods of persistent inflation, nominal income rises without tax rates necessarily being adjusted accordingly. The taxpayer thus faces a gradually heavier tax burden on the same amount of real income.

With the exception of the Netherlands, income tax was never as all-embracing on the Continent as it is in the United Kingdom, Ireland, or the United States. On the other hand, value-added tax (VAT) flowered in the European Economic Community before it crossed the Channel. VAT, however, is almost as comprehensive, in many ways more so, than income tax. While the percentage of the population of the European Economic Community countries that has to file VAT reports is smaller than those expected to file voluntary income tax assessments, VAT must be added to every transaction.

Without the full cooperation and collaboration of virtually the entire adult society, neither tax is enforceable. It is equally impossible to turn an entire population or even a fair percentage of it into effective criminals. This is one of the serious dilemmas the subterranean economy poses to modern society.

One of the more markedly ambivalent approaches to the subterranean economy comes from the western trade unions.* In theory, they strongly believe in and support tax law enforcement and should encourage the Internal Revenue Service and similar bodies across the Atlantic to maintain proper staffing, so that the taxes due from big business and the upper income brackets is collected in full. In practice, however, the trade unions have, in recent years, come to realize that fiddling with the tax returns is a national, cross-class pastime, which more of their members, in numbers though not in amounts, probably engage in than any other sector of the economy. The Swedish unions, among the most progressive in the world, have been wrestling with this fact for some time. Unions in other western democracies, less candid, have been uncommonly quiet, for once offering no advice.

Distances between the various western European centers are, of

---

* A far larger percentage of the labor force in the European Common Market countries and Scandinavia are unionized than one would find among their American counterparts.

course, much shorter than in the United States, and the practice of transferring undeclared income across borders to havens such as Switzerland, Luxembourg, and smaller countries in relatively close proximity is recognized and frequent, as is that of changing one's official residence. But the proceeds of most unrecorded transactions remain within the country in which they were earned. Some are kept in cash or used as a complementary source of family expenditure; the rest, in part laundered, are saved and applied to investment. Bigger sums are often more simply laundered by being moved across borders.

Undeclared funds first deposited in Switzerland, for instance, are brought home and then invested as equity or long-term loans under a bogus foreign name. Diamond merchants and polishers have, in recent years, increasingly resorted to this method. Not everyone who launders funds derived from the subterranean economy does it by moving them in and out across international borders. In countries where lotteries are legal, such as Italy, France, and the United Kingdom, people attribute capital increases to having drawn a lucky number. In some cases, an active trade exists in which the real winner in a lottery sells the coupon to somebody who feels the warm breath of the authorities down his or her neck and believes it is worthwhile legitimizing his or her unmeasured capital. The seller may not find ownership of covert funds (with a certain premium added) so embarrassing.

In Greece, southern Italy, and some other places, the tradition of buying brides is used to launder previously unrecorded capital. Leaders of feminist groups are pushing hard to legislate against this custom, but years will pass before it dies out.[1]

Another form of laundering but more risky is the discovery of some "legacy" from a remote source, vaguely documented and difficult for the authorities to track down.

Early in 1981, greater public recognition of this phenomenon was expressed in a series of publications throughout the Common Market. One article pointed out that "Moonlighting [is] an indicator of hyperdevelopment." It was devoted to discussing two recent works on the subject, published in French.[2] A March 3 article in *The Times* was headed, "Tax collectors ask for more staff to tackle black economy"; and "Black economy can be beneficial" (discussing a report prepared by the Institute for Fiscal Studies) headed an article that appeared in *The Financial Times* on March 4. Then, on March 6, *The Herald Tribune* headed an article with "Hidden economy: safety valve for West? Recession modifies official attitude on moonlighting."

The emphasis of these articles and papers has been on cottage industries and retail mom-and-pop business evasion. They rarely mention any of the larger-scale avoision practices. One reads of plans to strengthen systems and to hold conferences on the subject in Europe, while the British appear to be less concerned by this economy and its continuing growth in the coming few years may be expected.

THE UNITED KINGDOM

The notion of mischief thrills and shocks the British. They are delighted to talk of it. In recent years, the use of the term mischief is common in talking of avoidance: how it tampers with the national accounts or with the fair distribution of the tax load. They may also blame mischievous avoision for hindering the pursuit of a coherent national economic policy and for preventing it from being implemented smoothly, efficiently, and successfully.

In the decade leading up to 1978, British sterling lost more than two-thirds of its purchasing power. Now, how did that effect the individual? A single person earning £5000 in 1967 was liable for an average direct tax rate of 32 percent, with a marginal rate of 37 percent. In 1977, assuming the same individual's gross earnings were pegged to inflation, on an income of £15,000 his or her average tax rate would have been 46 percent and the marginal tax rate would have risen to 70 percent. To maintain his or her real take-home pay in 1977, a gross salary of £23,600 would have been required, or, just to keep pace with inflation after tax, a real increase before tax of over 50 percent. Effective rates rise in periods of inflation automatically, without legislation. The passive official stand of the government on this has a depressing influence on the average- and higher-income earner. The automatic, inflationary increases of tax rates on honest earnings certainly sweeten the attractions of avoision.

From 1960 to 1975, public expenditure in the United Kingdom as a percentage of its gross national product increased from

41.2 to 61 percent. In the same period, the gross national product grew, in constant figures, by close to 50 percent.[3]

This rise in expenditure was explained by the increased appetite of the administration.

During the same period, in real terms, the British government more than doubled its social security and national health service budgets; that for education increased by somewhat more than double and that for housing more than trebled, but in no way could the British imperial bureaucracy prove that the extent or quality of the service it supplied corresponded to such a rise.

Not all public employment is negative nor is all private enterprise constructive. As economic pressures increase and, with them, unemployment in the private sector, we have been witnessing a slow growth in public employment. Here, more often than not, no objective measurements are taken of the efficiency of the labor employed while, in the private sector, where the decline of profits is one yardstick, dismissals and redundancies have been kept on, increasing unemployment. Some of those laid off have since joined the subterranean unreported economy. Between 1954 and 1974, total public employment increased by 13 percent,* while that of the private sector dropped by 1 percent. Since then, the increasing rate of unemployment indicates further drops in published figures reporting on the private workforce.

It is the abuse of welfare and social services and an overweening bureaucracy that are the substantial factors giving moral support to tax evasion. One can understand the argument that people who work for their living productively are entitled to keep what they earn, rather than pass some of it on to various parasites on society. The greater degree of acceptance and tolerance toward avoision is more than a gut feeling; it is authenticated in a survey carried out in the fall of 1976 by the Institute of Economic Affairs in London. Three-fifths of the survey's sample of 712 persons agreed with the view that "if people want cash rather than checks so that they do not get taxed, then good luck to them." Nearly 70

---

* In spite of more than halving the British Armed Forces. The main demand for additional public employment came from the local authorities, the staff of which grew during the period by 78 percent.

percent also believed it was not right that they should pay tax on what they earned in their spare time, while just over half did not see why they should declare income from personal and domestic services when they know others do not. There was a marked reluctance to condemn people who do not declare income received from providing personal services. The institute concluded that the survey revealed a degree of tolerance toward evasion that probably did not exist toward any other form of illegal activity.

The London Times, summing up a leader, added the warning that the same conditions which breed the subterranean economy have an ill effect on society as a whole. They engender corruption and all that that implies.

In the United Kingdom, taxation became a serious burden during World War II. But even during the decades following World War II, taxes on income, national insurance payments, and health insurance deductions continued to increase. Thus, compared to a total personal income of £17,628 million in 1957, tax, national insurance, and health deductions amounted to £2,259 million. By 1967, personal income had nearly doubled, reaching £33,435 million, while taxes and the rest had grown two and a half times, to just off £6 billion. Over the following eleven years until 1978, because of inflation rather than any increase in real production, total personal income reached £143 billion, while income taxes and the like came to nearly £30 billion. In the twenty-one years prior to 1978, nominal personal income rose just over 8.1 times, while income taxes, national insurance contributions, and health deductions grew by a multiple of over thirteen!

In this age of free or almost free exchange, most hard currencies can easily be carried across borders. In the United Kingdom, where such controls were only recently removed, businesspeople with unrecorded cash receipts could stash them away in a foreign bank where they could collect income without attracting the attention of the Inland Revenue Service. The tax dodger in the United Kingdom would, of course, have to check that he or she was not placing the money in a country that had an information-swapping agreement with his or her own and where the banks reported clients' income to their authorities. But, to date, even the Common Market taxpeople do not really work together so closely.

Kangaroo-style leaps in the amount of income tax paperwork

are not unique to the United States. Similar rapid proliferation can be seen in Britain. Comptroller and Auditor General Sir Douglas Henley reported early in 1980 that any large expansion of investigation work would mean more of a load for accountants than they would be able to handle.[4]

General awareness that something was wrong with the British tax system increased in the summer of 1979, when the chairman of the Inland Revenue Board, Sir William Pile, estimated that untaxed subterranean income may well have reached £10 billion sterling in 1978, or about 7.5 percent of the gross national product.[5] Convinced that Sir William was exaggerating, Kerrick Macafee, a British government statistician, published a paper[6] in which he claimed that the subterranean economy could not be more than 4 percent of the total gross national product. According to him, the only piece of statistical evidence we have on the size of the subterranean economy is the difference between two differently calculated gross national product totals. If one adds up the total amount people say they spend or save and subtract from it what they say they earn or raise otherwise (which is always less although the two should be identical), one should arrive at the figure of the subterranean economy. Some time later, Mr. Macafee was supported in his theory by the Institute for Fiscal Studies, which claimed in a paper that the subterranean economy was in the general range of up to 3 percent of the gross national product and usually contributed to the state of the economy.[7]

Early in 1981, Sir William was just as confident that his oft-quoted estimate of the unmeasured economy as 7.5 percent of the surface economy could well be on the conservative side. When he was in office in the late 1970s, he had his economists measure a number of models of British economic behavior. The findings indicated that the unrecorded proportion of income might reach 10 percent, but was probably nearer 7.5 percent, which figure he adopted. He accepts the theory that, while the surface economy of today is stagnant, the covert economy, with a vitality of its own, is growing, both independently and in relation to the economy as a whole.

The 7.5 percent avoision figure first put forth by Sir William became accepted in the early part of this decade. At the end of February 1981, the staff of the Board of Inland Revenue urged the British government to step up its fight against the subterranean economy and to assign more staff to block the tide.[8] They argued that the additional outlay would be justified not only because of the increased revenues to the exchequer, but because it would help keep public borrowing within limits without resorting to higher taxation.

The difference, translated into missing taxes, was computed[9] to be £2.7 billion for the year ended March 31, 1977. Compared to this figure, the £13.5 million (to which another £13.5 million should be added in the form of penalties and interest) recovered by the revenue services in taxes for that year represented a success rate of approximately one-half of one percent.

Both the British and the Americans tend to ignore extraterritorial economy. They feel more comfortable with a description of the hidden economy like Mr. Macafee's[6]: income hidden from official statistics, such as income undeclared for tax purposes and payment in the form of perks rather than cash. For them, the undeclared income of moonlighters and the self-employed seems the most important component of the hidden economy.

Another flaw in the British tax collection machine came to light in 1980: the abnormally high rate of error in assessments made by the British internal revenue staff. An in-house sample check made in June 1980 indicated that 27 percent of tax returns were incorrectly processed. In addition, 12 percent of codings were inaccurate and 24 percent of the returns contained errors. Sir Lawrence Airey, chairman of the board of Inland Revenue, attributed the errors in part to the pressures imposed by three finance bills which had been passed in 1977, changes in mortgage rates, and industrial action.[10] No doubt he is right, but they are also one more indication that the structure of the system is close to caving in.

As in the United States, the degree of tax compliance in Britain varies with the sector of the economy and the region. There is little doubt that in the farming regions of the United Kingdom less respect is shown for the income tax authorities than elsewhere. Mention has been made (see Chapter 7, p. 58) of how an unreported but active cash economy helps stimulate some of the officially poorer parts of England. Similarly, every Britisher knows that the official data for Scotland's beautiful counties describe poverty, lower wages than average, and an unemployment rate exceeding 10 percent. But, behind these figures, *The Economist* [11] informs us, the human truth is often more prosperous. The largest industry north of the border lies in the "penumbra of services related to providing Bed and Breakfast, and most of them avoid the taxman's eye. With the illicit whiskey still as its emblem, An Cor-Beothsklain Dhu—the Black Economy, has always been a healthy sector of the highland output. Dodging the Lairds or the excisemen is still fair game but there are newer pursuits. Far more fish are landed than officially sold."

THE SUBTERRANEAN ECONOMY IN ITALY, OR MIRACLES FROM MILAN TO MESSINA

In the European Common Market, possibly the most blatant example of the subterranean economy is Italy; one reads of virtually continuous economic and political crisis in that country. Yet, when traveling in northern Italy, between Rome and Milan, one sees prosperity and building construction left and right. One soon realizes that the people one meets are not law-abiding, taxpaying businesspeople, but hardworking entrepreneurs and laborers with a strong feel for free enterprise. According to Edward Harrison,[12] in spite of the fact that Italy's government was close to bankrupt, in 1978 that country imported more Rolls-Royces and caviar than any other Common Market nation. It was second only to Britain in its intake of French champagne and to France in its consumption of Scottish whiskey. The Italians have also bought the greatest number of rare furs and Cartier baubles. Harrison claims that all this is the result of a decision taken by a large number of Italians to ignore the tax inspectors in Rome and to run their lives in their own way.

As there is scarcely any credibility to Italian statistics, it is impossible to evaluate the official estimate that 6 million workers,[13] or one-third of Italy's labor force, are really employed in unrecorded industries. Whatever the precise figure, the consensus is that moonlighting is vast and widespread in Italy. It is of interest to note that the system is accepted by the trade unions and the Communist party; there is less labor unrest in clandestine businesses than in the larger industries of the open economy, like Fiat or government-owned plants. The presence of moonlighting provides the entrepreneur with a flexible labor force, willing to work overtime; it helps the small- and medium-size textile and leather industries in their competition with products from other western countries.

In Italy, through a simple marketing structure, the connections of the plant owner with the go-betweens and retailers make it fairly easy for him or her to reach the consumer, without the embarrassment of having to confront the authorities, who might demand the markup of value-added tax. Nobody seems seriously worried lest the power of the government to enforce law and order becomes stronger.

Barbara Shenfield refers to Dr. Antonio Martino, who described how the Italian undeclared economy effected an economic miracle, a victory for the people over their rulers and an example for other free nations to follow.

Italy's official statistics of economic performance are such unreliable indicators of the real economic condition of the country because upward of 25 percent of the economy is "off the books," operating outside the state-regulated revenue system. Many of the civil servants are among the leading moonlighters in Italy. Over half the government personnel has a second job: at the Ministry of Agriculture, the proportion reaches 68 percent.[14] An interesting fact is that approximately one-fifth of the Italian civil service hardly ever shows up to work, as there is no effective supervision or documentary control of their presence or absence.

The volume of unrecorded industry is significant not only for Italy but for the whole European Economic Community. *Time* magazine[15] quotes Naples Mayor Valenzi as having said that from his city, which has no registered glove factory, 5 million pairs are exported annually. The unmeasured Naples shoe industry is reputed to be just as large. In Milan, there are only 5000 homeworkers on the city's commercial register, while the real figure is estimated at 100,000!![16]

Perhaps general acceptance of the subterranean economy in Italy is best illustrated by press reports of a strike in Bari—of cigarette smugglers!

Statistics published by the Censis Research Institute* are also very telling: only about one official in five puts in a full work

* Censis: The Centre for Social Investment Studies. A politically orientated research institute close to the Christian Democrat party, the largest member of Italian coalition governments.

load of six hours per day; the average Italian civil servant works for one-third of the time—about two hours per day. Many show up to register and are then off to other business.

The Italian press began investigations of its own following the Censis study. *Il Messagero* headed its series of articles "A Voyage of Investigation Among Empty Desks."

When at work, government employees spend a considerable proportion of their office hours trading. One easy place to get contraband cigarettes, cosmetics, woolens, or other textiles free of excise in Italy is in the building of the Ministry of Finance.

There are those who rationalize their low work morale on the grounds of their substandard wages or the failure of government plutocrats to address themselves to the problem of discipline. This latter is certainly a factor contributing both to the general anarchy of the country and to the almost total disregard of the average-income earner for the national tax laws.

The official figures of the Italian economy are indicative of the collapse of both their macroeconomic data collecting system and their direct tax collection. According to published figures, the government budget, which constituted 20 percent of the gross national product in 1950, rose to over one-third during the 1960s and will reach 46 percent by 1980. Such an excess over the recorded increase in the gross national product is quite prohibitive. The proportion of direct taxation in total government expenditure during these three decades was always close to, but under, 20 percent.

It is sometimes said that the hidden economy distorts the picture of the size and health of the total economy. This is visibly true in Italy.

Louis Turner discusses the accounts of Italian corporations.[17] He tells us that Italian businesses may be worth ten times more than their books show. This disparity creates problems when a company changes hands. One of the ways in which to avoid huge capital gains taxes is to effect the sale via a subsidiary residing in a country where there is little or no capital gains tax. Alternatively, the services of a Vatican bank may be used.

FROM SCANDALS TO CORRUPTION AND ON TO THE SUBTERRANEAN ECONOMY

Not least among the reasons for the growing disenchantment of the European taxpayer is the increased feeling, often supported by evidence from the press or the courts, that corruption is rampant in the higher echelons of government and among th politicians of many western European countries. This is freely acknowledged to be the case in Italy, but the attitude has, to a certain degree, spread through France, the Benelux countries, and West Germany.

The largest scandal in Italy in recent years involving government officials broke in the second half of 1980. Its full ramifications are not yet known. But in jail as a result is retired General Rafaele Giudice, until 1978 the esteemed commander of the paramilitary Guardia di Finanza, the National Financial Police, once regarded as a bastion of rectitude. And even the martyred figure of former Prime Minister Aldo Moro was brought into the scandal.

The Inland Revenue Service knew what was going on, as well as the nationalized Italian refineries and their distribution corporations. The latter have been accused of falsifying outgoing documents so as to reduce taxes payable on refinery products. The amounts that should have been paid to the authorities during the 1970s but were not could total more than $2.2 billion!

The main beneficiaries were the leading Christian Democrat party and the smaller, often allied, Socialist party. What is unclear is what amounts were paid to which politicians. But that the money changed hands is undoubted.

The scandal became public not as a result of any government investigation, but because of the jealousy of some political faction which felt that its share of the loot was unsatisfactory.

A recent (1980) case in Belgium was that of S.A. Eurosystem, a small subsidiary company of S.A. Poudrières Réunies de Belgique (PRB), a manufacturer of explosives and a member of the Société Générale group, possibly the largest Belgian business corporation. The sole purpose of S.A. Eurosystem was to negotiate and sign a contract well in excess of $1 billion for a hospital project to be put up in Riyadh and other centers in Saudi Arabia. For various reasons, the deal collapsed and S.A. Eurosystem became insolvent; the extended debt, the very disappointing pace of construction, and the deferral of advance payments which the Saudis had promised to make all contributed to the bankruptcy. The economic and financial press began probing for answers to questions such as: How could an essentially empty company, with no resources of its own, obtain such a huge and, on paper, lucrative building contract? It was discovered that secret commissions and kickbacks totaling 27.5 percent of the face value of the contract had been paid out by Eurosystem in its bid to close the deal, and, further, it is believed that at least $8 million were distributed, in the form of commission, among worthy Belgians.

It is commonly accepted that paying bribes to foreigners, especially Arabs, east Europeans, or Africans, is an inevitable part of the cost western business has to bear if it wishes to conduct trade in these countries. When it turns out that some of this money is passed back by recipients to nationals of the contracting country, suspicions arise. Had the Belgian minister of finance, for instance, not ruled in advance that these commissions, a large proportion of which were paid to nonresident Belgian nationals, were made with the knowledge of the government and so recorded, a major tax fraud scandal could have developed. The affair gradually settled, but not before some Belgians had decided to include more of their income than previously in the unrecorded part of their economy.

In France, the question of how many diamonds former President Valéry Giscard d'Estaing received from erstwhile Emperor Bokassa, and how much they were worth, remains unanswered. The former French president never denied the charge of the deposed emperor, but sources close to him alleged that it was exaggerated. In May 1980, however, he used the provisions of a 1963 antiterrorist security act to detain for six months, without trial, a certain Roger Delpey, who had been given documents by the former African ruler that could have cast light on the affair. During his detention, his "diamond documents" were removed from his police dossier and the French court agreed that they need not be presented as evidence at his trial, if and when it ever takes place.*

---

* Explanations offered by the former president during his election campaign of what actually happened to the diamonds left many people unconvinced.

Not all cases of modern-day corruption involve such high-ranking officials. There is a convenient gray area which, together with some refinement and class, provides social pleasure and position as well. Commercial laws and licensing procedures are often cumbersome, frustrating, and time-consuming, unless palms are greased. In today's society, in which government is responsible for huge budgets, senior ministry officials and the ministers themselves become familiar and friendly with the business executives such as the suppliers to their ministries. It is quite common, on both sides of the Atlantic, for government bureaucrats to spend their vacations as guests of the businesspeople who require their goodwill. The head of a Belgian pharmaceutical corporation, for instance, will host the minister of health at his Bermuda hideaway, in the expectation that the processing of a new production line will be licensed more quickly. There is a tacit understanding, not an overt, cut-and-dried quid pro quo arrangement, and, naturally, the vacation expenses are tax deductible.

This give and take has a cumulative effect on the average citizens. Without formulating a clear ethical judgment, they begin to feel that the tax system is, perhaps, unfair, that politicians and those close to government get a better tax deal than they do. When all is said and done, perhaps they owe it to their family and to themselves to pay as little tax as possible.

FRANCE

Similarly barefaced in their uncooperative approach to the tax authorities, the French are almost as direct as the Italians about their subterranean economy. France is a country with a highly organized bureaucracy and indirect taxes such as VAT which, in theory, should help trip the fiddler, but it is common practice to dodge the French VAT.

In volume, possibly the largest single outlet of the French subterranean economy is extraterritorial, especially the service given by Switzerland and its banking facilities. Also popular are property and other long-term investments outside France. One encounters it when:

- Senior business executives expect to be paid some of their remuneration into a tax haven

- Preferred clients receive under the table commission kickbacks
- Part of the intercompany transactions are credited through a foreign country
- Securities and futures are traded in the name of nominees

A survey conducted long, long ago mentions that in France a spot-check by inspectors showed that 85 percent of those living on "sundry income," such as retired people, file returns well below their real income.

Unrecorded labor has contributed materially to the construction of highrise buildings in cities from Paris to Nice. It has penetrated not only agriculture, other forms of heavy physical work, and communications, but also the realms of beauty parlors and clerical services. Thanks to the unrecorded economy, rates of remuneration have improved, with employer and employee sharing the amount of tax avoided or saved between them. "If I were to declare the work of a translator, it would cost me 5000 francs and he or she would get only 3500 francs, net. I would rather give nothing to the tax collector and pay him or her 4200 francs."[18] Then, as in Germany, the *gastarbeiter* is quite an important element, the laborer with no work permit, willing to take cut-throat wages.

One-quarter of France's 25 million labor force is thought to engage in moonlighting; it is estimated that income tax returns should be for half as much again as they actually are.

THE BENELUX COUNTRIES

In the Benelux countries, the relative extent of the unmeasured economy is probably not smaller than in Britain or the United States. Tax evasion in Belgium doubled in the second half of the 1970s and is estimated by Professor Max Frankel to stand at approximately B.Fr. 200 billion.[19] According to him, income tax evasion from funneling money out of the country is the most common form of tax fraud, closely followed by ignoring inheritance taxes, while failure to report on real estate transactions comes in third.

Not to be left behind, a Dutch report shows that two out of three who could do so, chose to evade tax.[16] In an earlier study, out of 901 men and women asked, 54 percent believed that all taxable income should be declared, but 31 percent thought it all right to leave some undeclared. There was another 8 percent who thought the individual should pay no tax at all (7 percent gave no answer). It is interesting to note that, as in other countries, the younger respondents condoned evasion the most.

The Dutch approach to the social welfare state, big government, and high taxation is comparable to the social philosophy of the Swedes. Together, these two peoples lead the West in size of government expenditure as compared to gross national product. Both legislatures are aware that levels of direct taxation cannot be raised any further. In both countries, while there is a certain amount of flexibility in indirect taxes such as value-added tax, any additional expenditure will be financed by new public debt. Not surprisingly, they have, in recent years, become very much aware of the dynamics of their growing subterranean economy. The subject has become popular both on the academic level and in the news media. There is, for instance, the Van Bijsterveld Report concerning tax evasion,[20] prepared at the request of the minister of finance by Professor W. J. Van Bijsterveld, one-time commissioner of Internal Revenue in Holland. His very serious presentation does not omit some lighter glimpses, such as the fact that, somewhere in Holland, moored on one of the rivers, there is a yacht called "Black Money" bobbing alongside her sister boat, the "Dame Blanche." In a more sober vein, he points out that it is evident that an evader will generally try to get out of all taxes possible, not only direct income taxes and related burdens, but also VAT and other indirect taxes. He, personally, does not believe that a lighter tax burden would reduce avoision. He recommends strengthening the fisc by imposing heavier punishments and shaming those found guilty: exposing them in public. He believes that standards of tax audits can be raised and that, if audit procedures are revitalized, the pace at which assessments are issued can be speeded up. An important point he makes is to reduce to the minimum the burden of paperwork and other inconveniences to those who pay their taxes in full.

Other research,[21] backgrounders, articles, and television appearances have generated considerable interest.

The Dutch are aware that notaries, who are bound by law to disclose illicit transactions, invariably draw up secret addenda to contracts for the sale or purchase of real estate, in which unreported cash markups are noted. When asked whether, in doing this, they are not laying themselves open to blackmail, their answer is that they would be out of business if they did not cooperate, as everybody does it. In an effort to keep monies so gained within Holland, the Dutch government now markets unregistered, negotiable bearer bonds, which are quite anonymous.*

The solution commonly accepted in Holland is to increase, indeed double, the number of tax staff, and attempts to recruit new tax inspectors are probably more imaginative in Holland than in other countries. Promising young men and women are given free university training plus salary during their studies and are not bound to any minimum period of service thereafter. If they do decide to take up government positions, they earn relatively well per net working time, probably better than their independent counterparts, and their positions are more secure. In spite of these incentives, the number of those leaving the Internal Revenue Service is always higher than that of those entering.

Taxation and social security payments rose in the Netherlands from an average of 18 percent of the gross national product between the two world wars to some 35 percent in the 1950s, then to 45.3 percent in 1970 and close to 55 percent in 1978. These figures refer to the measured economy. They do not take into account the unmeasured part, estimated by Professor Heertje[22] on the basis of what is essentially anecdotal evidence rather than precise measurement at equal to 20 percent of the gross national product, and growing at a lively pace.

BELGIUM

In Belgium, the undeclared economy is probably just as rampant as in Holland, and, in one aspect at least, more problematic. In both countries a substantial part of the monies derived from the unmeasured economies are deposited abroad, in Switzerland, for instance. A fair amount of that originating in the Netherlands is laundered there and then returned to its country of origin in the form of a foreign investment. Not so

---

* Several other countries do the same. Possibly the most attractive deal is that offered by the Israeli government, which issues debentures pegged to the consumer price index, thus allowing subterranean funds to be linked.

in Belgium, where political instability is increasing and pessimism about the future is considerable. Funds transferred out of Belgium are usually kept there. Belgian importers and exporters find it wise to leave funds abroad. The importers do so by arranging with their foreign suppliers to mark up (slightly) the cost of the imported goods. Exporters from Belgium do not note in their books the full proceeds of their sales. Dominant among the latter are the Antwerp diamond merchants and industrialists, members of one of Belgium's largest industries. (See also Chapter 8 on diamonds.) There is no sign of proper auditable books of account. Workers in shipyards and ship maintenance, another big industry in and around Antwerp, feel similarly justified in disregarding Belgian tax laws.

A Belgian professor of accounting has pointed out that "tax evasion is no longer regarded as a criminal offence by large segments of Belgian society." The reasons he gave were similar to those of citizens of other countries with big-budget governments:

1. Government's failure to cut its expenses
2. Dramatic increase in the complexity of the tax system, making it virtually impossible for the average citizen to comply
3. Cynicism of Parliament and the politicians, with their double standards about salaries and perks
4. Ineptness of bureaucracy and common knowledge that kickbacks are widespread
5. The extreme liberality of the social security system, which permits the waste of public funds

As in neighboring countries, the Belgian authorities are not making serious plans to reduce the impact of the covert economy or even taking steps in this direction.

The subterranean economy is rampant throughout the Common Market. It is just as extensive in Germany, Denmark, and Ireland, the other veteran members of the European Economic Community, and the anecdotal evidence is that it is complementary in these countries to that of its neighbors. The measured economies of such incoming and future members as Greece, Spain, and Portugal are less developed, probably comparable with the Italian economy, as is the far larger unrecorded element in these countries.

Just as the member countries have failed to react, to date, to the presence of the subterranean economy in their countries, there is no sign that any politician or functionary of the Commission headquarters in Brussels or in the Parliament of Europe, in Strasbourg, is planning to approach the subject and tackle it as a problem to be resolved by the community.

REFERENCES

1. See also "Divorcing the Dowry," *International Herald Tribune,* November 21, 1980, p. 20.
2. Intersocial No. 61, June 1980. Commission of the European Communities: *le Travail Marginal et Clandestin en France, au Royaume Uni et en Italie,* Study No. 79/42 and *Problèmes Politiques et Sociaux* Number 400, l'Economie Souterraine, published by Documentation Française, October 24, 1980.
3. Blue Books on National Income and Expenditure (through IEA Readings).
4. See "MP Spells Out New Tax Avoision Scheme," *Accountancy Age,* February 22, 1980.
5. "Exploring the Underground Economy," *The Economist,* September 22, 1979, p. 106.
6. Kerrick Macafee, "A Glimpse of the Hidden Economy," *Economic Trends No. 316,* November, 1979.
7. "Black Economy Can Be Beneficial," *The Financial Times,* March 4, 1981.
8. "Tax Collectors Ask for More Staff to Attack 'Black Economy' and Save the Treasury £3000 M," *The Times,* March 2, 1981.
9. Tom Bingham, *Tax Evasion, the Law and the Practice,* Alexander Howden, London, 1980, p. 7.
10. "Tax Collectors Ask for More Staff to Tackle 'Black Economy,'" *The Financial Times,* June 5, 1980.
11. *The Economist,* May 31, 1980, p. 81.
12. Edward Harrison, "How Phantom Workers Produce the Good Life," *Now,* September 21, 1979.
13. *U.S. News and World Report,* October 22, 1979, p. 53.
14. "Nur Menschen," *Der Spiegel,* November 1980, pp. 194–195.
15. "Credibility Is at Stake. A Financial Time Bomb Threatens the Community of the Twelve," *Time,* January 19, 1981.

16. Raffaele de Grazia, "Clandestine Employment: A Problem of Our Times," *International Labour Review,* Vol. 119, No. 5, September–October 1980, p. 550.

17. Louis Turner, *Invisible Empires,* Hamish Hamilton, London, 1970, p. 77.

18. L. Gazzo, "Travail Noir: Les Chômeurs Vocent Rouge," *Vision,* Paris, April 1977, p. 36.

19. *The Financial Times,* March 20, 1979.

20. W. J. Van Bijsterveld, *Aangepaste versie ven het Verslag van de belastingfraude,* Holland, April 1980.

21. At the end of 1980, for instance, Professor Arnold Heertje, together with Harry Cohen, published *"Het Officieuze Circuit," een Witboek over Zwart en Grijs Geld.*

22. Ibid.

13

DIFFERENT SOCIOPHILOSOPHIES, DIFFERENT SOCIOECONOMIES

COMBATING COMMUNISTS

There is subterranean economic life, in varying degrees, in all democracies, but there are Sovietologist economists who claim that it is even more developed in totalitarian states such as the Soviet Union, Poland, Rumania, and other Communist countries.

The eastern European countries are not burdened by a heavy tax system, but they suffer from a far cruder, authoritarian style of government inefficiency than does the West. It is, therefore, not surprising that, while no statistics or articles are published on the subject, anyone who visits behind the Iron Curtain soon discovers the vital life signs of a vigorous subterranean economy. A friend returning from a visit writes that "if you want anything done properly or any sort of service in Russia, considerable cash bribes or presents of goods have to accompany the request." In Rumania, a common practice is to do jobs badly during the regular working day because wages are very low, and to moonlight in the evening. As there is no direct taxation in these countries, it is not tax evasion that is the predominant reason for such moonlighting, but rather, it is another example of people working in their own best interests to obtain a standard of living commensurate with their own requirements for leisure time and other factors. All this, however, is totally illegal. For those caught, punishment can, in theory at least, be very harsh. Yet moonlighting is not the only unrecorded form of economic activity behind the Iron Curtain. Farmers, for instance, fail to market their products through official party agencies. Officials, both in the bureaucracy and in industry, expect and receive kickbacks for a good part of the transactions carried out in their areas of responsibility. The laws of the eastern European countries stipulate heavy punishments for anyone caught operating on the black market, profiteers, and white-collar criminals, but little publicity is given to legal trials for financial crime. Petty evasion is almost encouraged. Most governments in the Communist bloc, aware that they cannot effectively prevent the continuation of the subterranean economy, prefer to turn a blind eye and are content if it operates in an orderly fashion.

In the very heart of Moscow and other large cities in Russia—sometimes on the premises of top-ranking state industries—entrepreneurs of all ages live dangerously by employing dozens of artisans to produce better manufactured clothing, leather goods, and other commodities in public demand. Unknown to the authorities, they are very private underground millionaires. If caught, they will be sentenced to extensive prison terms in Siberia.*

In every one of the larger cities of the Soviet Union, foreign summer tourists can witness what is clearly an improvised open-air minimarket, with farmers and small artisans trading their wares, rather than marketing them through state channels. One can see travelers from the Volga Basin and as far away as Baku in the Caucasus who finance their trip to Moscow by two valises of early spring vegetables or simple trinkets for sale in such open-air markets. Further off the beaten tourist track, high-spirited barter of merchandise goes on. Nobody is sure whether or not the authorities will suddenly change their minds and crack down on the traders.

Periodic announcements of severe sentences, sometimes capital punishment, passed on persons "discovered" participating in the black market do not seem to deter this form of

---

* Konstantin Simis describes corruption in the Soviet Union in his *U.S.S.R., the Land of Kleptocracy,* published in the spring of 1982 by Simon & Schuster. An excerpt appeared in *Fortune* on June 29, 1981, pp. 36–50.

underground economy. On the contrary, the markets are thriving.

They do so in spite of what seems to people living in the free society a frightening and cruel form of government. They do so because they have broken through the barrier of fear and found that the risks are well worth taking.

The Communist party has always had teams of people monitoring and infiltrating various objectives in the West, trying generally to manipulate them. It is not surprising that the heads of the Kremlin have become interested in the international comings and goings of the hidden economy and have, in their plodding way, begun seeking to exploit it for their own ends.

Thus, it is of interest that Communist banks are becoming increasingly active. They are even trying to attract custom from the capitalist world. Numbered bank accounts, for instance. Since the early 1970s, Hungary's National Savings Bank has offered to hold foreign currency accounts on behalf of foreign nationals. The accounts as advertised have distinctly bourgeois characteristics:

- Secrecy
- State repayment guarantee
- Tax-free interest
- Unchecked disposability by depositors

The bank claims to have about $5 million deposited in this way. Not a very large amount compared to Switzerland or even considerably smaller havens, but still a point of interest.[1]

LATIN AMERICAN ANARCHY

When undeclared monies are transferred across international borders, they can create economic facts and pressures of their own. Active, venturesome entrepreneurs may find that the pace at which they accumulate funds is faster than their capacity to place them discreetly for further growth within the borders of their own country, especially if it is small. If they decide that it is wiser to smuggle them out, they may discover, after a time, that more of their capital is invested abroad than at home and that it is prudent to follow the money. Thus, Latin Americans find themselves in Europe or North America, just as Israelis end up in California and South Africans in London.

It is very common for the Latin American owners of medium and large businesses to deposit some of their savings in offshore banks in the Caribbean or Switzerland. It is not often noticed that U.S. banking facilities in New York, Los Angeles, or some other southern city, especially Miami, are now among the major outlets for funds smuggled illegally out of Mexico, Venezuela, Brazil, Argentina, Chile, or some other South or Central American country.

Most major international banks, headed by those of the United States, are aware of the dangers, such as the embarrassment of being caught aiding the smugglers, but also of the considerable rewards of doing business in Latin America even if there it is considered to be illegal. They have developed competitive instruments, close to the Latin American countries, to cater to the funds coming from them. Nearest are the Dutch Antilles, but, in recent years, others have grown rapidly, including the Cayman Islands and the Bahamas.

In Spanish- and Portuguese-speaking South America, implementation of the direct income tax laws is not generally very effective; indirect sales taxes are similarly evaded. Many South American countries suffer from chronic inflation, and people who accumulate liquid funds prefer to keep them in a harder currency than their own. Pressures to rid themselves of local currency in favor of the U.S. or Canadian dollar, Swiss or French franc, German mark, or Japanese yen are considerable. The local administrations have, however, over the years, developed clear and, in theory, severe foreign currency controls. In many of these countries, the purchase of hard currency is forbidden and most is bought illegally.

Still at an early stage of economic development, a substantial part of the potential labor force of many of the Latin American nations has not yet been recorded. National statistics do not take them into account. In part, the people are very poor, living in ghettos like those around Mexico City and Rio de Janeiro or in far-off corners of their countries. When they find gainful employment, they pay little heed to official regulations and laws, and the large-scale entrepreneurs seeking a cheap labor force are aware of this.

The system is run on the same principle as the subterranean economy in northern Italy, Tuscany down to Rome, but the workers in Latin America are far more exposed to sudden, unforeseen circumstances.

Publications indicate that when the middle classes in Chile, Mexico, and Brazil feel that the income tax rates are too high and consequently unjust, they believe they have a moral justification for evading. This view is strengthened when they observe the misuse or improper application of public funds and, for his or her resolution, the tax evader often enjoys public sympathy.

In Chile, generating the unrecorded economy are the small retailers who usually trade with little or no documentation, often in cash. The larger-scale merchants, seeking market outlets, are delighted to use the small retailer as an excuse for the absence of proper documentation.

Evasion is so common that it is roughly estimated that some 80 percent of the citizens do not pay the taxes due. Even the director of the Chilean Inland Revenue Service acknowledged[2] that his staff estimated that at least 30 percent of income tax due was missing as a result of tax evasion.

Venezuela is far richer and economically more advanced. But evasion is just as rampant.

In an age when certain industries and other components of the economy receive preferential status, incentives are frequently offered to new investments, usually in the form of tax relief. The purpose may be either to attract foreign capital or to raise more local money. With government playing an increased part in the economy, directly or through nationalized bodies, it often partakes in the new investments and then claims the benefits due to such enterprises. Basically, these tax holidays or grants are a legitimate, even encouraged, form of avoidance. In some countries government presence can be overwhelming. The Venezuelan government, for instance, either directly or through its vast number of government-owned industries, is the biggest single employer in the country. Unlike truly free private enterprise, most of its companies are exempt from direct taxes and from most indirect taxes as well.*

---

* The existence of the subterranean economy in Venezuela is no secret either to government or to the public.

The public feels dissatisfaction with what it believes are the improper activities of politicians, invariably smoothed over when discovered. No big fish ever gets punished, certainly not sent to jail, so why file an honest return or pay taxes, asks the average person.

Early in July 1980, the most influential Caracas newspaper quoted a well-known member of the opposition as having said that some Venezuelans declare only 10 percent of their real earnings. There are no exchange controls and monies are continuously being shipped out of the country. Part of it, once whitewashed, returns for local investment in the form of a "foreign loan." Tax evasion is recognized as a fact of life, neither condoned nor condemned. The low tax morale and the incapacity of government is freely, frequently, and openly discussed. The most common vehicles through which earnings are funneled are the many foreign banks operating in Venezuela.

The unmeasured economy is well entrenched throughout Latin America. Long before Arab sheiks became the latter-day oil moguls, Spanish-speaking land, mine, and business magnates were pouring funds into tax havens and other forms of refuge in that continent. The Latin American economies may be less developed than those of the West but, as contributors to the unrecorded international scene, they were pioneers.

THE INDIAN EXPERIENCE

The third world countries are also affected by the subterranean economy. Most are corrupt autarchies, with the exception of India, now the largest democracy in the world and the poorest; but, whatever its form of government, kickbacks and bribery have always prevailed.*

In 1972, an Indian government committee enquiring into direct taxes concluded that the effects of black market money on the economy could be described as disastrous, but little has since

* They were prevalent throughout the British Empire, right until it disintegrated after World War II. The British Raj might punish harshly those natives found guilty by the courts of taking bribes, but he did nothing to prevent the practice and, in fact, often encouraged corruption. Very few of the British colonies knew how to eradicate or reduce this unpleasant legacy of colonial days after they achieved independence.

been done to reduce the power of the Indian underground economy.

On July 27, 1980, *The Times* of India indicated that the black economy had assumed enormous proportions. It set out to prove, by describing the threefold rise in the prices of real estate in Delhi and Bombay, the intensive jewelry business (Bombay has, in recent years, become one of the world's diamond centers), and other developments, that the new and growing fortunes must have been made outside the law, since it is impossible to become rich in India within the law.

According to *The Times,* much of the reason for the vitality of the black economy is that the political parties are financed out of its funds, and the businesspeople financing the parties expect an immediate payoff for their "donations."

The Indian government is different in many ways from its counterparts in the West: it is, for instance, vitally interested in the underground economy and has conducted investigations into the subject.* And there are those who understand that rigid economic controls and tax rates of over 95 percent feed the black economy, that it is imperative to move, as soon as possible, toward a more liberal fiscal system. The difficulty is that the Indians find it hard to translate their conclusions into effective programs.

In India, where the population is half of the democratic world, government has enacted a huge bureaucracy, supported by a prohibitive network of rules which it has absolutely no chance of enforcing and which are virtually ignored by the general public. In the *Business Standard* of Calcutta for Saturday, September 13, 1980, D. K. Rengnekar speaks of the sad fact that the black economy has taken over and almost drowned the official economy. He blames this widespread malaise, which has turned India into a sick society, on the "fantastic" complicated web of bureaucratic controls which debases values and drives heretofore honest people to despair and corruption. Given its present size and growth rate, the restrictive credit policies of the India Reserve Bank have proved to be totally ineffective.

---

* It is food for thought that only where black money has become the dominant feature of the economy is it sufficiently recognized to be spoken of in full seriousness in public.

Financed by taxes and borrowings, over three-quarters of the investment in industry in India is made by the public sector. Yet, government-owned enterprises remain inefficient monstrosities—capital-intensive and, at the same time, hopelessly overstaffed. By comparison, Indian free enterprise is highly sophisticated, but, to a large degree, within the realm of the subterranean economy. The honest businessperson in Bombay who earns an 8 percent return on assets of $250,000 will have it virtually *all* taken away by income and wealth taxes, plus a compulsory deposit. Wealthier entrepreneurs, if honest, could face a negative net income. Not surprisingly, almost all wealthy Indians have taken their economies underground, often bribing politicians and tax inspectors as they go.

On a purely academic level, the Indian situation is empiric proof of the Laffer curve, which shows that where tax rates are very high, tax returns are very low. On a practical level, the Indian scene is one of chaos and anarchy, endangering the continued security of the democracy. Foreign currency controls will have to remain in force in India in the foreseeable future, but reducing the official tax burden might introduce a challenging new economic approach. Unfortunately, there is no sign that either Mrs. Indira Gandhi, without doubt the most powerful person in India, or any other leading figure has any practical plan to change the ways of the Indian economy. The difficulties and challenges facing India are so enormous that it may take some time before the presence of the subterranean economy can be seriously lessened.

WELFARE AND OTHER DEMOCRACIES IN EUROPE

Austria

One of the countries which, de facto, encourages the development of the subterranean economy is Austria. It is led by Finance Minister Hannes Androsch, who, at forty-two in 1980, was a veteran with twelve years' experience in his post. He claimed that "it is more important to bolster the Austrians' confidence in their money than to collect one or two billion more schillings in revenue." He winked at the fiscal sin most appalling to his peers: income tax evasion. And, seemingly to this end, the banking law was clarified in 1979 to confirm the legality of "anonymous accounts" so secret that even bank employees need not know the names of the depositors.[3]

It is possibly not coincidental that in the second part of 1980 the West learned of the biggest financial scandal in Austria of recent years. It was an affair that had been brewing long, full of allegations and insinuations but with few hard facts, and it concerned the construction of a large hospital in Vienna, with huge budget overruns, kickbacks, and conflicts of interest. Mr. Androsch appeared to be connected with the case. He had remained a partner in his auditing firm while he was in government office, and one of the other partners in the firm was directly involved in the consulting to the hospital and was exposed in the Austrian press.*

Sweden

The public sector in Sweden produces 65 percent of the gross domestic product. This means that it contributes more to the gross national product** than the public sector of any other western nation—even if the Dutch are breathing hard down their necks. The appetite of the Swedish imperial bureaucracy remains insatiable although the forty-four–year tenure of the Social Democrats ended in 1977 and a liberal-conservative coalition now heads the government. It may, in theory, be committed to the "little person," but it nevertheless has increased its presence in the economy, with direct income tax pretty well as high as the administration believes it can effectively be. In September 1980, the Riksdag, in its quest for more sources of income, voted to increase value-added tax to 23.46 percent—the highest rate in Europe. Since that autumn,

---

* Afterward, Mr. Androsch came in for a considerable amount of flak in a series of articles describing his ostentatious, expense-account lifestyle until, as 1980 drew to a close, an effort was made to brush up the image of the Social Democrat party and its leader Bruno Kreisky; a bruised but wiser and, probably, wealthier Hannes was forced to retire as minister of finance and, probably, from his political career.

** According to *U.S. News and World Report* of October 22, 1979, Sweden has a hidden economy that equals 10 percent of the official national output; it costs the government in lost taxes an amount equal to 15 percent of the budget. If these figures are not exaggerated and if the amounts had been incorporated in the computations of the Swedish gross national product, government expenditure would be marginally lower than 60 percent of the gross national product.

there has been a very noticeable reaction and pressure to stop increasing public expenditure. But, to date, no government effort has been noticeable, nor have there been any energetic legal or other steps toward reducing the government budget.

Swedish government protection of ailing industries is far more pronounced than that of, say, Chrysler in the United States. In a single year, for instance, the shipbuilding industry was subsidized by the equivalent of nearly $5 billion, plus more than $15 billion in the form of guarantees.

Those worried about the size of the Swedish subsidies have computed that the average taxpayer provided a thousand dollars in aid to the shipbuilding industry and the cost of maintaining each individual employee in the industry averaged $125,000! Upon hearing of these and similar absurd-sounding economic measures, many Swedes decide to try to disassociate themselves from them in future.

In Sweden today, the subterranean economy is fatalistically accepted as being very active. In a survey carried out in the Stockholm area, it was found that about 10 percent of the contractors did not have records with the income tax authorities. While in theory there is a requirement to deduct tax at source on payments made to various types of artisan, in fact there remains the double price quote: one with documents and tax deductions, the other for work without. In the shipyard industry, it is quite common for subcontracting teams to "disappear" on completion of their contract, only to reemerge in a marginally reorganized form at a neighboring yard. There appears to be little antagonism to this avoision. Possibly, the one aspect that is really bothering the members of the overt, legitimate economy is the unfair competition of those who practice in the subterranean economy.

Only in 1978 did the income tax authorities inform the politicians of the magnitude of the subterranean economy. They were surprised and disturbed. What probably shocked the Swedish politicians most was to hear that data presented to them was based on a survey in which 19 percent acknowledged that they had never (or only in part) declared their taxable income. The parallel figure for a similar survey carried out in Oslo, capital of Norway, was 25 percent. Other statistics put the figure at only 16 percent for all of the population of Sweden. As in other countries, the precise figure remains an educated guess at best.

Sweden has gone further than other capitalist countries toward a managerial society. The power of the civil service and the executives in the large free-enterprise concerns is substantially more than that of the disappearing entrepreneurial society. Most politicians who move into elected positions are ex-civil servants who still believe that big government is the right way. If it is not working as well as it should, that is the result of human error and can be corrected. The majority of the opinion-formers in the media and the government concur with this view. If there is a subterranean economy and its size is 10 percent or more of the total gross national product, ways should be found to reduce it and, preferably, eliminate it completely. After repeated attempts to squash covert production by means of tax controls among the toughest in Europe, the Swedish authorities seem to be fighting a losing battle. Still, there is no school of thought that says that the tax level of the budget should be reduced.

Specialist teams composed of lawyers, sociologists, and economists, close to government and the major political parties, are planning how to improve compliance, how to close loopholes and make the tax collector's work more efficient. And, as a result, in 1979 the income tax offices, with a larger appropriation, increased their annual audit from 10,000 thousand to 15,000.

Still, the subterranean economy not only perseveres but is probably gaining ground. Very few Swedes believe that even if such an unlikely event as a tax cut were to occur there would be a drop in avoision. It has its own dynamics, which push many people who might otherwise feel uncomfortable about it into creating undeclared sources of income for themselves. This vicious circle is fostered by the Swedish banking system, in which the pace of turnover and paperwork is such that the authorities cannot enforce the kind of reporting that would match documents and cause discomfort to those in the subterranean economy. Not surprisingly, the regular, average "legal" person asks himself or herself more often than before why he or she should carry a full tax burden when the big cats escape the net to the south of France or just manipulate the law without moving so far from home.

There are various specific Swedish subterranean characteristics—Swedish sailors and many laborers in their shipyards, for example, refuse to accept vouchered, documented, tax-deducted wages. In the spring, as many Swedes prepare their boats for the coming season, many car owners or operators discover their automobiles "develop" battery trouble. Upon the advice of their garage mechanics, they replace the batteries, install new ones in their cars, and place what are really only partly used batteries in their little motor boats; these will last the summer.

Sweden still has currency exchange controls. But it is suspected that most medium and large businesses have unreported assets, operating in other parts of the world.

Since the year from 1977 to 1978, the macroeconomists in Sweden have realized that there is an increased gap between the details collected for the purposes of national statistics and the facts on a microeconomic level. The material collected showed that Sweden was experiencing a recession and that bankruptcies should be expected, though as yet no unusual business collapses have occurred.

The behavior of the subterranean economy in Norway is similar to that in Sweden, if somewhat more moderate. Moonlighting is common. Barter is probably increasing. Value-added tax, at 20 percent, is an incentive to both seller and buyer to practice evasion: the seller enjoys the bonus of not declaring the profit for tax purposes, while any normal buyer is happy with a 20 percent reduction.

Switzerland

Outsiders often hear of the stringent Swiss economic secrecy laws and their supervision by what is believed to be a competent police force. Stories abound of foreigners who have (sometimes inadvertently) crossed swords with the authorities and then spent many months, sometimes years, in Swiss prisons. It might be thought that these examples would be a deterrent to the indigenous Swiss. Yet, recent investigations tend to indicate that this is not so; that, for the Swiss citizen, the barrier of fear has all but disappeared with the growth, in recent years, of bureaucracy, bigger government, and higher tax rates than those of a generation or two ago. As in other countries, the concept of true progressive taxation, so essential to the practice of income tax, has long since been dropped as an ideology. Income tax is, at the moment, actually repressive.

Although it is still common for the ordinary Swiss to squeal to the police when they learn of the misdeeds of their neighbors and they are openly encouraged to do so, more of them than ever are opting to keep part of their earnings as unrecorded income: not only the moonlighting artisan and waiter, but also members of the more sophisticated professions, such as the accountant, the lawyer, and the banker, all of whom are, in theory at least, liable for quite considerable taxes and punishment if caught. Their involvement with the secret accounts of their clients, sometimes numbered, yields them hidden, undocumented income.

The bigger banks offer their staff perks and goodies ranging from in-house sports facilities to attractive holiday programs—all untaxed. Jealousy of these and other forms of conspicuous consumption is spreading as more and more people opt for avoision. In Switzerland, one hears of professionals confiding that they keep part of their income in the dark. "It may be regarded by some as an economic police state but they appear to have two sets of priorities—they are not exerting themselves in an effort to prevent their own subterranean world of avoision."

Switzerland is no welfare state and there is no evident poverty. Having had a considerably lower income per capita than, say, Sweden or Denmark in 1945, their standard of living more than caught up with the Scandinavian countries by the 1970s. With a considerably lower administration presence and lower tax rates than, say, Scandinavia or the United Kingdom, the Swiss subterranean economy is also believed to be smaller. The Swiss are reputed to act by the book. That means that nearly everybody, including the *gastarbeiter,* is careful to record all his income, even from moonlighting. The Swiss government is less intent than other democracies on including all the population in its bear hug, but it naturally is committed to upholding Swiss law and will, therefore, do all it can to confine the hidden economy to the fringes of society. As a result, it is believed that the lower tax rates still offer incentives to ambitious young people eager to better their lot and become rich. Few, if any, people in Switzerland are ashamed to try for wealth, nor are they branded for working too hard. With plenty of job opportunities, the less wealthy can look after themselves without resorting to transfer funds.

Few even among moderate European socialists would claim that the quality of life in Switzerland is worse than in any other European democracy or that the lot of the Swiss poor is materially harder. On the other hand, it could be argued that because the subterranean economy is far smaller in Switzerland than elsewhere in Europe, the Swiss socioeconomic infrastructure is under considerably less pressure than that of, say the European Economic Community countries and the United States.

REFERENCES

1. "What Hungarian Account," *The Economist,* February 7, 1980, p. 6.
2. In an interview published in the local magazine *Ercilla* on November 30, 1979.
3. "Austria's Youthful Finance Minister Gets Good Results with Novel Policies," *The Wall Street Journal,* July 3, 1980, p. 20.

14

IS THERE A WAY TO REDUCE THE SIZE OF THE SUBTERRANEAN ECONOMY?

"Most Italians have very little contact with the usually inept, always incompetent government officials, but those who have are not angry with the plutocrats, they are furious with them," commented Massimo in Rome. What he cannot forgive is the total inefficiency of his corrupt bureaucracy, as if there is no fair return for the bribes given.

To a large extent, those queried in other countries had the same reaction. "As long as heads of government, their ministers and senior civil servants continue to abuse their expense account privileges," says Sven-Erik in Sweden, "the negative publicity generated by conspicuous misuse of their government retreat (or yacht) for the benefit of family or friends will accelerate the decision of many members of the general public to move into the covert economy and, once there, to stay."

"We are living in an age of two-digit inflation and maintaining our standard of living is no mean feat. Paying income tax as required by law is bad enough but, in inflation, taxes are raised all the time without any law being passed, as we are pushed into higher income tax brackets. It is unforgiveable that we cannot get any more protection from government," complained Peter in Ireland. And indeed, while it is difficult to quantify its precise effect, modern inflation has contributed materially to disenchantment with government.

Today, one oft-mentioned solution to rising evasion is to simplify the system and to reduce taxes to a greater or lesser degree. This would reduce the inordinate amount of time devoted to the question of when does income arise and to whom.*

Although it has other positive attributes, the adoption by the Reagan administration of the Kemp-Roth bill to reduce tax rates by 30 percent over a three-year period will, probably, not be a big enough step forward.

The question is how much of a reduction is necessary. Even if marginal tax rates were reduced from 70 percent to 40 percent, it is doubtful whether evasion would lessen significantly. Most of the members of the subterranean economy today have no intention of budging from the semiovert, semicovert world in which they are living. If a few are ready to stand up and be counted, the majority will probably still hold back. They have adjusted to their way of life and its comforts, suffer no moral or ethical pangs, and have no interest in haggling as to what the optimal tax rate should be to get them back into the fully overt economy.

In the 1790s, William Pitt the Younger reduced customs duties with the aim of reducing smuggling and corruption. To some extent he succeeded. In 1933, the U.S. Congress decided to repeal Prohibition and legalize trade in spirits. And a practical decision it was, too; it put a stop to bootlegging. But it is difficult to imagine the disappearance of evasion until a different standard of taxes is introduced, with less bureaucratic interference and a lowering of expectations from government. Governments in the past generation have promised too much and delivered too little. Arthur Seldon[2] has said that "if we are forced to pay by taxes instead of by prices we shall have less—of education or anything else—than we should like to have and are willing to pay for. Payment by taxes—the financial mechanism of State education and the Welfare State—prevents us from doing as much in welfare as we wish and can. . . . Ordinary people will pay more for a service if they can see their families will benefit than they will in taxes

---

* J. E. Meade, who headed a committee in the United Kingdom, wrote that by reducing all income tax to a single, moderate flat rate, the administration of the present system could be simplified out of all recognition and much complicated legislation would become redundant.[1]

for a service in which they can see no benefit for higher tax-payments."

The rapid expansion of government in the postindustrial economy, and that of the economy itself, led to the growth of the subterranean economy. Today, when the amount of intangible, as compared to tangible, commodities produced and traded is continuously increasing both in volume and in value, it is becoming harder and harder to measure them objectively. Indeed, objective methods of monitoring the very existence of intangible commodities are decreasing and, in many cases, disappearing. It is something of a paradox that, to avoid reporting and taxation, it is easier to barter intangibles than visible goods which have usually been recorded somewhere at some time, as part of someone's inventory.

Then there are offshoots of the manufacturing industry—the proliferation of architects, corporate lawyers, and a widening galaxy of other types of specialists and consultants. Few of these professionals go wholly underground, as some of their clients file at least a good part of their receipts for their own tax requirements, but many have ways of receiving additional, what would have been heavily taxed, income by methods undisclosed to the fisc.

There is less security in the unrecorded economy, though the risk deters fewer than one might have expected.[3] Within the laissez-faire atmosphere of the subterranean economy, it is virtually impossible for either customer or worker to take out an insurance policy against disaster. Members of the subterranean economy have no protection against acts of God. The laborer is not covered by social security or medical insurance; the businessperson cannot sue for damages; the small-scale bribery which accompanies any illegal activity flourishes.

Then, there is the resentment of members of the legitimate economy who feel that they are being exploited by government while their neighbors earn untaxed or unrecorded income and, at the same time, at least some of them receive dole and other social security benefits.*

---

* Barbara Shenfield writes how government and society "Do not (always) discriminate between moonlighters who want to keep what they earn, and welfare cheats who draw both benefits and wages and other figures on the shadier fringes of behaviour. . . ."

Tax evasion is nowhere close to the violence of other crimes such as acts of terror, murderous assault, or grand larceny. Yet, not least because of its subversive elements, its impact on our way of life could be greater. Whatever the laws of any particular country, liberal or radical, however effective the administration, it is virtually impossible to have a 100 percent law-abiding population. There will always be an anarchistic element, trying to take the law into their own hands. Modern society can live and thrive only as long as the activities of this minority are not really significant and can be contained in proportion to the nation as a whole, both materially and socially. The subterranean economy will continue to thrive as long as:

- Government spending remains as inefficient as it is today
- The authorities do not acknowledge that it is a far more serious social malady than they are prepared to admit
- The administration cannot come to grips with it or legislate only laws supported by the majority of the population
- It is so widespread socially and so generally condoned

As the 1980s begin, the financial literature is, for the first time, giving thought and space to the subject. But the political establishments do not seem to have yet fully realized the debilitating effects of the subterranean economy.

Most official or quasiofficial organs in the West are content to repeat the idea that with a larger budget, stiffer punishments, a bigger effort, and better education, the tax authorities will succeed in cracking down on illegal labor. They must be dreaming.

To alleviate the maladies of the covert economy, we should probably aim at more socially acceptable standards, including both a scale of taxation that people can accept and, no less important, a changed standard of social norms.

Persuading the members of the subterranean economy to change the climate and their mores is a labor beyond the capabilities of even the most herculean technocrat working alone. It will require a whole new set of expectations from society as a whole, both from government and from itself.

Today, only lip service is paid to the ideal of "government of the people, by the people, for the people."* Communal tasks should be fairly distributed, and all members of our free society should share them. Those who wish to uphold and perpetuate democracy must very soon address themselves to the task of rethinking and revising their countries' tax systems and reformulating the scope of government responsibility for and interference in the privacy of the individual. Only with a much smaller government presence is there any chance of reducing the size of the subterranean economy.

REFERENCES

1. See J. E. Meade, *The Structure and Reform of Direct Taxation,* George Allen & Unwin for the Institute of Fiscal Studies, London, 1978, p. 316.
2. Arthur Seldon, *Charge,* Temple Smith, London, 1977, pp. 67 and 75.
3. "Make the Best of the Black Economy," *The Economist,* June 30, 1979, p. 73.

---

* Emphasis over the years has changed. Whereas once the main aim really was "for" the people, the words "by" and "for" may today be interpreted to refer to the relatively high percentage "of the people" working within the civil service.

APPENDIX

Forms Generally Required to Be Filed by a Sole Proprietorship Conducting Business in New York City*

---

* Current regulations as of June 1981.

Agency	Type of Form	Reporting Form Number	Annual	Semi-annual	Quarterly	Monthly	More Frequent than Monthly	Other	Remarks
Federal	Individual Income Tax	1040	X						
	Individual Estimated Tax	1040 ES			X				
	Application for Federal Identification Number	SS-4						X	Upon inception of business
	Payroll Tax Return	941			X				
	Payroll—Annual	940	X						
	Payroll Reconciliation	WRS-2			X				
	Payroll—Annual Reconciliation	W-3	X						
	Withholding Deposit	501			X				
	Unemployment Deposit	508			X				
	Miscellaneous Income	1099 MISC	X						Filed with government and a copy to all persons receiving income from business
	Summary and Transmittal of Information Returns	1096	X						"
	Statement for Reconciliation of Non Employee Compensation	1099 NEC	X						"
	Statement for Reconciliation from Profit Sharing	1099 R	X						"
	Statement for Reconciliation of Health Care Payments	1099 MED	X						"
	Statement for Fishing Boat Members	1099 F	X						"
	Wage and Tax Statement	W-2	X						Filed with federal and state governments an[illegible] a copy to employee

	Employee Allowance Certificate (withholding)	W-4	X						Copy in business files and copy, depending on exemptions claimed, sent to government
State	Individual Income Tax	IT-201	X						
	Individual Estimated Tax	IT-2105			X				
	State Payroll Tax	IT-2101	X	X		X	X		Frequency of filing depends on amount withheld
	Reconciliation of Payroll Tax	IT-2103	X						
	Report to Determine Liability under Unemployment Insurance	IA-100						X	Upon inception of business
	Unemployment Insurance Tax	IA-5			X				
	Certificate of Registration for Sales and Use Tax	ST-105						X	Upon inception of business
	Sales and Use Tax	ST-100	X		X				Amount of taxable receipts determines frequency of reporting*
	Non Resident Allocation of Withholding Tax	IT-2104.1	X						Kept by employer
	New York State Sales and Use Tax Estimate	ST-800						X	Annual estimate could be required depending on receipts
	New York State Annual Wage Statement	IT-2102	X						Copy to recipient of income

* In addition, there is in excess of 15 separate forms substantiating exempt use or special treatment of a transaction under the sales and use law. Records must also be maintained of sales to customers in approximately 70 different taxing jurisdictions.

Agency	Type of Form	Reporting Form Number	Annual	Semi-annual	Quarterly	Monthly	More Frequent than Monthly	Other	Remarks
	New York State Annual Information Report	IT-2102.1	X						Copy to recipient of income
	New York State Transmittal of Information	IT-2102.4	X						
	New York State Statement for Recipients	IT-2102P	X						Copy to recipient of income
City	Individual Unincorporated Business Tax	NYC-202	X						
	Individual Unincorporated Business Tax Estimate	NYC-5UBTI			X				
	Commercial Rent and Occupancy Tax Questionnaire	RG-1						X	Upon inception of business
	New York City General Occupancy Report	OTX	X						
	Commercial Rent Tax—Quarterly	CRQ			X				
	Commercial Rent Tax—Annual	CRA	X						

Source: Compiled by Arthur Gelber, Laventhol & Horwath, Certified Public Accountants, based on regulations as of June 1981.

INDEX

ABOUT THE AUTHOR

Dan A. Bawly is an Israeli CPA with extensive business contacts in the United States, Europe, and other parts of the world. He is executive partner of Bawly Millner and Company, one of Israel's largest firms of CPAs and a member of Horwath & Horwath International. He travels frequently and, over many years, has gained a first-hand view of the economic mechanisms of many of the western democracies.